The Elder Japanese

Karen C. Ishizuka

with the Assistance of

Michiko Peters
Tsuruko Hasson O'Mary
and
Linda Grauberger

Center on Aging, San Diego State University

The Elder Japanese

A CROSS-CULTURAL STUDY OF MINORITY ELDERS IN SAN DIEGO

Editor & Project Director:	Ramón Valle, PhD
Project Director:	James Ajemian, PhD (First Year)
Associate Editor:	Charles Martinez, MSW
Secretaries:	Mrs. Peggy King
	Mrs. Patricia Murphy
	Mrs. Alicia Nevarez-Krotky
	Ms. Cynthia Wright
Cover:	Mr. Calvin Woo, Humangraphics
Published By:	Center on Aging
	School of Social Work
	San Diego State University
Design Style & Phototypeset:	Betty R. Truitt
	Word Processing Center
	San Diego State University

Monographs and Technical Reports Series

The Elder American Indian:	Frank Dukepoo, PhD
The Elder Black:	E. Percil Stanford, PhD
The Elder Chinese:	Ms. Eva Cheng, MSSW
The Elder Guamanian:	Wesley H. Ishikawa, DSW
The Elder Japanese:	Ms. Karen C. Ishizuka, MSW
The Elder Latino:	Ramón Valle, PhD
	Ms. Lydia Mendoza, MS
The Elder Pilipino:	Ms. Roberta Peterson, MSSW
The Elder Samoan:	Wesley H. Ishikawa, DSW

Project Supported by Funds from U.S. Department of Health, Education and Welfare, Office of Human Development, Administration on Aging. Grant Number AoA-90-A-317, Mr. David Dowd, Project Officer AoA, OHD, DHEW.

ɯy The Campanile Press, San Diego State University

Library of Congress Cataloging Data
Catalog Card No.: 77-83483
Ishizuka, Karen
The Elder Japanese
San Diego, Calif.: Campanile Press
p. 71
7708   770708

ISBN 0-916304-36-1

Distributed for the Center on Aging by
The Campanile Press
San Diego State University
5300 Campanile Drive
San Diego, California
92182

/K. C. Ishizuka|

Acknowledgments

The research team extends grateful acknowledgment to the many individuals in the San Diego Japanese American community who played both major and minor roles in the conduct of this project. A partial list of persons who lent considerable consultation include: Sakiko Akita, Donald Estes, Reverend Shinichi Fukiage, Jack Hamaguchi, Reverend Harry Hashimoto, Mas Hironaka, Reverend Yoshi Kaneda, Reverend Scott Madison, Kaz Mizuno, Roy Muraoka, Reverend Koju Terada, Mrs. Koju Terada, Tom Uda, Reverend James Toda, Mrs. Yoshimi Ueji, and Vernon Yoshioka.

As is documented in this report, the involvement of these and other persons was vital to the project from beginning to end, making it truly a shared responsibility. Hopefully, this research endeavor will further their shared goal of enhancing the San Diego Japanese American community.

There are also a number of other persons who have had varying degrees of impact to the project as a whole from the proposal stage to the end. Dr. Gideon Horowitz was instrumental in developing the proposal for which initial funds were received. Dr. James Ajemian assumed the directorship for the project during its first year. Mr. Charles Martinez provided extremely helpful technical support throughout the process of the research, especially at the point of finalizing the monographs. Dr. Roger Cunniff, Mrs. Sharon Swinscoe and Mr. Gerald Thiebolt of The Campanile Press were most helpful in extending their assistance throughout the process of publishing this editorial serial of reports. The researchers are equally appreciative of the continual support from the Administration on Aging by Mr. David Dowd, Project Officer. We wish also to recognize the School of Social Work of San Diego State University under whose general auspices the study was conducted.

We are grateful to all of the above for their involvement in this research effort.

/K. C. Ishizuka

Table of Contents

I.   INTRODUCTION TO THE STUDY

This study of Japanese American older persons is part of a larger study on ethnic minority older persons residing in San Diego, California. The study as a whole, extended over a two-year period between 1974 and 1976 and was funded by the Administration on Aging, Office of Human Development, Department of Health, Education, and Welfare.

Research Objectives

The research was undertaken with the following three objectives in mind.

- First, to analyze characteristic lifestyles and customs, as well as the primary interactional networks of ethnic minority groups and in this case, especially those of Guamanian elders.
- Second, to explore and delineate the perceptions and viewpoints of the Guamanian elders toward formal programmatic assistance and human service networks with the overall intent of tracing, where possible, the interactions between the formal programs and the primary networks.
- Third, to test out a methodology appropriate to obtaining information about ethnic minority populations and specifically the elders of these populations.

To a large extent the third objective of the appropriate methodology guided the first two objectives of gaining a better understanding of ethnic minority lifestyles and assessing the impact of these lifestyles on the level of their knowledge and utilization of service agencies. From the researchers' standpoint, the methodology to be utilized was as critical as the actual information which would be obtained. The reason for placing such importance on the research approach was twofold. First, it was the result of the researchers' evaluation of previous data gathering efforts within ethnic communities. This evaluation provided information about the importance of such factors as community involvement when engaging in research efforts. Second, the reasoning was based on the call from both ethnic minority researchers such as Romano (1969), Takagi (1973), and Vaca (1970) and ethnic majority investigators such as Blauner (1972) and Moore (1971, 1973) for fresh perspectives and research approaches to the issue of ethnicity.

Study Populations

Besides the Japanese American component, the other ethnic group components of the study included: American Indians, blacks, Chinese, Guamanians, Latinos, Pilipinos, and Samoans. Each ethnic group component functioned as a unit with its own research coordinator, interviewers, and subsequent monographs.

In view of the diversity of the overall study population and the upper limit of the study size ($N = 628$), strict proportional representation of the Third World populations in San Diego could not be achieved. In accordance with the methodological approach utilized, the choice was rather to proceed with purposive samples in order to approximate ethnic content representation. The numerical breakdown of the study population is provided in Table 1.

Table 1

Study Population by Ethnic Group Components

$n = 628$

Group	f	%
Latino	218	34.7
Black	101	16.1
Pilipino	74	11.8
American Indian	62	9.8
Japanese	60	9.6
Chinese	50	7.9
Samoan	40	6.4
Guamanian	23	3.7

Elders in San Diego

The participants in the study all resided in the Standard Metropolitan Statistical Area (SMSA) which encompassed San Diego County. As of 1975, San Diego had an estimated 1.5 million residents, of whom approximately 13.2 percent or 198,300 persons were estimated to be aged 60 and above. See Table 2.

Table 2

San Diego SMSA Population Under and Over Age 60

$N = 1,500,000$

Population age	f	%
Under 60 years	1,302,000	86.8
Over 60 years	198,300	13.2

SOURCE: San Diego County Area Agency on Aging, updated 1975 estimates.

Of the estimated 198,300 persons over 60 years of age, 22,000 (11.9 percent) have been classified as persons of ethnic minority groups. Table 3 summarizes the available breakdown by ethnic group of persons over 60.

/K. C. Ishizuka|

Table 3
San Diego SMSA Age 60-Plus
Population Estimates By Ethnic Groups

Group	f	Percent of Total Age 60-Plus Population N = 198,300	Percent of Minority 60-Plus Population By Ethnic Minority Group n = 23,900*
Anglo/White	174,400	87.9	
Latino	14,900	7.5	62.3
Black	4,500	2.2	18.8
Pilipino	1,300	0.6	5.4
Japanese	700	0.4	2.9
American Indian	500	0.3	2.0
Chinese	300	0.2	1.4
Samoan	300	0.2	1.4
Guamanian	200	0.1	0.8
Other ethnic minorities not clearly designated	1,200	0.6	5.0

*NOTE: The Area Agency on Aging estimates of specific ethnic minority populations have been further updated with best estimates available from organizations serving each population.

In actual fact, the available census figures on ethnic minorities in the San Diego area are deemed highly undercounted by the ethnic communities themselves and therefore are considered invalid and unusable by the ethnic communities concerned.

II. METHODOLOGY

Overview

The research strategy utilized within the inquiry was based on the theoretical perspective of combining quantitative and qualitative research approaches so that the information obtained from close-ended questions would be placed in the context of the social environment of the respondent. The theoretical sets utilized in the research stem from Glazer and Strauss (1967), Campbell and Stanley (1963), Gouldner (1965), and Sieber (1973), who collectively propose alternative considerations for survey research. In addition, the direction for the research was drawn from Myers (1974) and Valle (1974), whose empirical research demonstrated approaches toward combining both quantitative and qualitative analysis.

Figure 1 highlights the data collection strategy. If the research approach could be summarized, it could be said to have been geared to the collection of what Cooley (1908) and other theorists have termed primary group behaviors against the backdrop of complex secondary social environments. With regard to the San Diego SMSA, these include mixes of ethnically different populations living in urbanized as well as dispersed and ruralized situations and all living in an equally complex network of systems and services. The questions asked by the researchers centered then both on obtaining indicators of ethnicity and primary behaviors in the context of their secondary group and interactional environments.

Figure 1
Overall Strategy for Data Collection

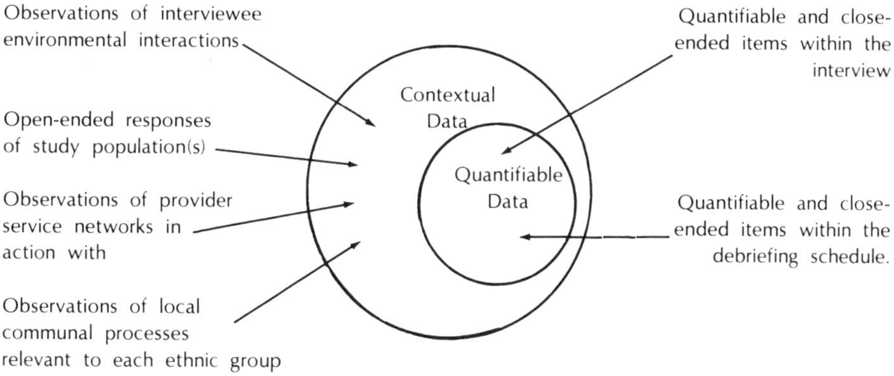

Observations of interviewee environmental interactions

Open-ended responses of study population(s)

Observations of provider service networks in action with

Observations of local communal processes relevant to each ethnic group

Contextual Data

Quantifiable Data

Quantifiable and close-ended items within the interview

Quantifiable and close-ended items within the debriefing schedule.

Community Involvement

An integral part of the research from start to finish was the involvement of the constituencies of the research. Individuals and groups from the local Japanese American community participated in the study throughout the life of the project, from the pre-planning stage through implementation of the interview process to the analysis.

Specific tasks in which community involvement played an important and active role include: (1) formulation of issues for problem definitions; (2) recruiting and screening potential interviewers; (3) training selected interviewers; (4) identification of potential interviewees; (5) brokering and communicating with regard to the study; and (6) analysis of findings.

Although the conduction of research in this manner has generous time and budgetary implications, research can only truly reflect the social reality of a group by being a shared responsibility between community and university-based researchers.

Population Selection

The study groups were selected on the basis of attempting to tap into the normal or ordinary relational patterns of the ethnic populations within the study. Because of the diversity of the ethnic components of the study and the fixed size of the interviews allowed for by the project, the total number of the Japanese American sample was set at 60.

Potential interviewees were selected from identification of older Japanese Americans residing in the San Diego area by key individuals of the community and also from organizational lists. The sample was selected according to the following criteria for representativeness: (1) geographical residence; (2) sex; (3) age (over 55 years); (4) country of birth—United States or Japan; (5) generation; and (6) distribution by group of reference and non-group affiliation.

Interview Strategy

Tied directly to the population selection was the research decision to proceed within what Myers (1974) termed the "unconventional survey research mode." This approach has several distinguishing characteristics. First, as Stebbins (1972) indicated, the interview is seen as a beginning interpersonal relationship. Second, the interview is directed by an open conversational approach, built upon the development of trust and confidence in the interviewer. The maintenance of the relationship and the conversational approach is seen as continuous throughout the total interview. Third, the strategy includes the incorporation of observational techniques wherein the interviewer observes the living surroundings and interactions of the interviewee. By design the interviews were seen as taking place in the interviewee's home. Fourth, at all points of the interview, the interviewer secures the consent of the interviewee to obtain information on an ongoing basis as appropriate throughout the interview process. The interviewer is mandated to be especially sensitive to obtain consent to more sensitive areas or levels of intimacy and to provide the option to the interviewee either to withhold answers or to terminate the interview. The culturally syntonic (appropriate) clues, both verbal and affective, which comprise the core of this approach were worked out in the training period, as well as in the debriefing.

Within this style of interviewing, primary concern is placed on the human exchange that takes place. In this manner, the actual interview may also become a channel for the life experiences and wisdom of the interviewees to be imparted to others.

By utilizing this interview strategy, the study sought to provide a true representation of the sample by tapping into what Spicer (1971) called the persistent identity system and what was referred to by Solomon (1974) as the ethno-system.

With regard to the notion of informed consent, it should be noted that the study was initiated prior to the promulgation of the Department of Health, Education and Welfare human subject research guidelines: *Federal Register* (1975). The informed consent procedures utilized within the study did conform to the option of modified procedures wherein the written consent of the interviewee is not required but respondents' rights to privacy and refusal to participate are clearly protected.

Interview Instrument

The interview instrument was designed as a guide for the collection of information. This type of instrument was selected in accordance with the conversational approach of the interview strategy mentioned above.

In practice, this meant that the interview guide would provide the interviewers with the basic items of information needed according to the major objectives of this study as outlined in Chapter I. For example, date of birth was needed, but the interviewers were trained to ask this question in the most appropriate way, depending on the interviewee. Therefore, responses were given according to the Western Calendar (e.g., July 19, 1890) or according to the ruling era of Japan at the time of their birth (e.g., Meiji 32).

Additionally, the instrument contained both open- and close-ended variables in keeping with the overall data collection strategy illustrated in Figure 1. In order to obtain insight into the ethnic lifestyle of the interviewees, the interviewers must be given open-ended access in relaying belief systems, values, and symbolic constructs in their own way.

Interviewer Selection and Training

The interviewers were selected primarily on the basis of ethnic compatibility with the sample to be interviewed. Ability to converse in both English and Japanese was also a required capability. The interviewers were screened into the project through a variety of ways. The coordinator held individual conversations with each potential interviewer and consulted with community groups and key individuals before final selection of the interviewers was made.

The formal training of the interviewers was conducted in a total of 28 hours. Training first took place within the total group of interviewers from each of the ethnic components involved in the study. Then training within each subgroup was conducted to establish a knowledge base of interviewing techniques appropriate to each ethnic group. Two pilot tests per interviewer were conducted as part of the training process.

Because of the interviewers' vital role in the research and their insight from having direct interaction with the sample under consideration, the three interviewers were retained during the second year of the project in a research analysis capacity.

Data Collection Procedure

Precontacts.

Pre-interview contact with potential respondents began with their receiving a letter in Japanese and English introducing the purpose of the research and requesting their involvement by participating in an interview. The letter was written on University letterhead in order to establish the sponsorship of the research and contained the signatures of leaders of Japanese American organizations actively involved in the study. The letter informed the potential respondents that a bilingual, bicultural interviewer would call to answer any questions and to set up the appointment for an interview at their convenience.

The interview process.

The interview process itself followed the approach previously discussed. The actual interview was seen as a relatively long interpersonal exchange and was approached from the perspective that it could be a pleasant experience for both respondent and interviewer. The opportunity for the interviewer to accept refreshment, if offered, was provided for as fitting into the cultural style of the respondent. The interviewer was encouraged to engage in social conversation at the beginning in order that the respondent could become better acquainted with the interviewer and the purpose of the study. Termination of the interview was likewise to be conducted with respect to the interpersonal exchange that preceded.

An allocation of ten dollars per interviewee was made, which was put in an envelope with a Japanese card as an expression of appreciation on behalf of the Research Institute. This card was given to the interviewee or placed on a nearby table at the end of the interview, along with verbal expressions of thanks and leave-taking. The honorarium represented an in-kind exchange to the interviewees for his or her time and information.

Recording and coding.

The interviewers were encouraged to record all contextual data that would assist in providing a holistic picture of the person interviewed. Open-ended responses were recorded in the language used by the respondents and in as much detail as possible. The interviewers were also trained to record any additions to the close-ended items or conversation that might have been shared in the course of the interview.

Information from each interview was transferred from the interview guide to a code sheet for processing. This was accomplished either by the interviewer or by the coordinator during the translation of the interview responses. Both respondents and interviewers were given numbers, thereby eliminating identification of the interviewees by name.

Debriefing.

Debriefing sessions were held by the coordinator with each interviewer regarding the content and style of the interviews they conducted. The intent of these sessions was to supplement the coded data with contextual data in the form of observations, impressions, and conversations in order to provide an overall picture and feeling for the person interviewed.

Individual debriefing sessions were first held after each interviewer had completed two interviews. Subsequent debriefings were held with each interviewer at mutually acceptable times after completion of three to five interviews. Ample time for debriefing sessions was planned as they often included translation of Japanese concepts into English phraseology.

Analysis of Data

The analysis of the data was seen as a mesh of both quantitative and qualitative approaches. With regard to the quantitative data, the Statistical Package for Social Sciences (SPSS) computer program format was employed. For the purposes of the monograph level of reporting, frequency distributions and percentages were seen as the most appropriate. For purposes of the major project report, which compares intergroup variables, statistical measures ranging from analysis of variance and factor analysis were seen as applicable. In all instances, the quantitative analysis was to be played against the backdrop of the ethnic-environmental context in which it was obtained.

Preliminary analysis of data began during the debriefing sessions discussed above. Primary analysis was conducted by the coordinator and during a series of meetings of the research team, which consisted of the coordinator and the former interviewers who were retrained as research analysts. Together, this team approach put the statistics and figures together with the contextual data from the debriefing sessions into a meaningful overview of the sample studied. Findings were then presented by the research team to a meeting of leaders and community workers in the San Diego Japanese American community for their comment and discussion before being finalized. Analytical input therefore orginated from three sources: (1) the coordinator, who had primary responsibiltiy for the research; (2) interviewer-analysts, who had direct contact with the interviewees regarding the study items; and (3) community leaders and workers who have an on-going relationship with Japanese American older people in San Diego.

Expected Outcomes

The expected outcomes of the research were cast in terms of the three principal study objectives: (1) to trace the respective cultural patterns of the ethnically varied study population; (2) to delineate the respondents' outlooks toward formal services and networks of services; and (3) to test an alternative data-gathering methodology.

It was expected that the study as a whole, including this series of monographs, would provide findings to impact the field of aging at four levels:

(1) with regard to direct services and programs for ethnic elders, (2) with regard to policies affecting minority seniors, (3) with regard to the training of professionals to serve in the field of aging, and (4) with regard to further research in the field of ethnicity and aging.

/K. C. Ishizuka|

III. FINDINGS

A Profile of the Japanese American Study Group

Age, sex, and marital status.

The Japanese American sample consisted of 60 persons between the ages of 55 and 94, with the mean age being 67.5 years. There were 33 (55 percent) male respondents, and 27 (45 percent) were female.

Table 4

Sample Characteristics by Age and Sex

$n = 60$

| Age | Sex | | | | Total | |
| (in years) | Male | | Female | | | |
	f	%	f	%	f	%
55-64	16	27	11	18	27	45
65-74	9	15	6	10	15	25
75-84	6	10	8	13	14	23
85-94	2	3	2	3	4	7

Of the total sample, three-fourths were married. Of the remaining quarter, 18 percent were widowed, 5 percent were divorced or separated, and 3 percent had never been married.

Language.

Japanese was indicated to be the language of first priority for over half (57 percent) of the sample with 43 percent of the respondents listing English as their primary language. The majority (72 percent) responded that they could "get by" speaking English. A lesser number (58 percent) responded that they could "get by" using forms written in English. Only 1 respondent said that he/she could not "get by" speaking English, while 10 percent replied that they could not "get by" using forms written in English.

Educational levels.

All of the interviewees reported having had some formal education. Years of education ranged from 2 to 17 years with the mean being 9.8 years.

Employment and income.

A little over half (52 percent) of the sample studied were currently employed. Of those employed, most (65 percent) were employed full-time and 35 percent were employed on a part-time basis. Occupations most cited by the men were: (1) gardener, (2) farmer, (3) fisherman, and (4) nurseryman. The data indicated that most men have held more than one occupation during their working lives.

Occupations commonly held by the women included: (1) working in a cannery or garment factory, (2) helping their husbands with the family farm or business, (3) semiskilled labor (e.g., seamstress), and (4) office/clerical work. Eleven percent of the women identified themselves as housewives.

Sixty-five percent indicated their financial position as "fair," 28 percent as "good," and 7 percent as "poor." Because of the personal nature of this topic and the cultural orientation to underplay hardship and also underplay success, the data that was accumulated reflecting actual income is considered highly unreliable. The average monthly income ranged between zero and $2,833, with a mean of $618. Primary sources of income were Social Security (52 percent), and salary (40 percent). It is known that some potential respondents declined to participate in this study because of what they felt were poor financial positions.

Housing.

The majority (82 percent) owned or were in the process of buying their houses. Only 5 percent rented houses or apartments and only 3 percent of the sample were living with their adult children.

Activities.

Data on activities engaged in by the sample indicated a wide range of recreational pastimes. The three most frequently mentioned activities were gardening, 25 percent; knitting/sewing, 15 percent; and fishing, 10 percent. Other activities engaged in included sports, 17 percent; Japanese hobbies such as writing poetry (haiku and tanka), flower arrangement (ikebana), painting (sumie), and doll-making, 10 percent; and television/radio, 6 percent. Almost two-thirds of the leisure time activities the sample was engaged in were reportedly engaged in by themselves, with 7 percent engaged in with friends and family.

Origins and Residency Patterns

Of the total sample, half were born in the United States and half were born in Japan. Of those born in Japan, the length of residency in the United States ranged from 5 years to 74 years, with the mean being 54 years. For the entire Japanese American sample, years lived in San Diego ranged from less than 1 year to 67 years, with the mean being 39 years. Length of time in their present neighborhood ranged from less than 1 year to 59 years, with the mean being 21.5 years.

Length of time lived in the same house or apartment ranged from less than 1 year to 20 or more years. See Table 5 for length of time in present house/apartment.

Table 5

Length of Time in Present House/Apartment

$n = 60$

Length of Time	f	%
1-5 years	13	21.7
6-10 years	3	5.0
11-20 years	18	20.0
20+ years	26	43.3

Expressed Needs

General.

When asked to identify general problem areas, half of the respondents replied that they had none. As can be seen from Table 6, the three most frequently expressed problem areas include transportation, inability to speak English, and finances.

Table 6

General Problem Areas $n = 60$

Areas	f	%
None	32	53
Transportation	10	17
English language difficulty	5	8
Finances	4	7
"Have to make the best of it" (shikataganai)	2	3
Loneliness	2	3
Neighborhood safety	2	3
Moral changes in society	1	2
Tiredness	1	2

Health.

Half of the sample reported their health as "good," 42 percent "fair," and 8 percent "poor." Forty-five percent reported having been hospitalized as older persons and that they received the care they needed when hospitalized. Health problems reported are represented in Table 7.

Table 7

Health Problems Reported $n = 35$

Health Problems	f	%
Hypertension	13	37.0
Arthritis	9	26.0
Heart Problems	5	14.0
Vision	4	11.5
Ulcers	4	11.5

According to the data, the majority (93 percent) of the sample were familiar with Medicare, but less than half (43 percent) utilized Medicare. A little over half (52 percent) indicated familiarity with MediCal and only 7 percent indicated ever having used MediCal. In assessing the significance of these statistics, it must be noted that difficulty with the English language may have confused this data. It is conceivable that respondents utilize Medicare or MediCal without knowing or calling them by such labels.

Nutrition.

Regarding the number of meals eaten per day, 77 percent replied that they had 3 meals a day, 18 percent had 2 meals a day, and 3 percent ate 4 or more meals per day. Seventy-seven percent ate a mixed diet of Japanese and non-Japanese food, 17 percent ate primarily Japanese food, and 7 percent ate mostly non-Japanese food. Fifty-two percent usually ate their main meal with one other person, 22 percent ate with two to four others, 17 percent ate alone, and 8 percent ate with more than five people. Eighty percent of the sample required no special diet.

Transportation.

Primary means of transportation was the automobile (88 percent), with 8 percent utilizing public transportation. Sixty-seven percent drive their own car, and 23 percent rely on another person to drive. The majority of the respondents (97 percent), replied that transportation was usually available when needed.

Kind of help needed but not available.

When asked their opinion of kinds of help that were needed but unavailable, one-third of the respondents replied that they didn't know or hadn't thought about it. Eight percent replied "none." Of those needs expressed, data indicated that the primary need was for a Japanese convalescent, nursing or retirement home for the elderly in San Diego (36 percent). Other expressed needs included transportation, 15 percent; recreation, which included Japanese movies and social center, 9 percent; and bilingual services, 6 percent.

Japanese retirement home in San Diego.

At the request of some members of the San Diego Japanese American community, a question regarding the favorability of a retirement home for Japanese in San Diego was included. The majority (72 percent) responded positively to this idea, 12 percent responded negatively, and 16 percent gave no opinion. Of those who reacted favorably, some felt it was a matter of great priority and would personally utilize one. Others were less enthusiastic and replied that they would use it if necessary or that they themselves were taken care of but knew of others who would need and welcome one. Of those who responded negatively, responses included opinions that it wouldn't work and also emotional feelings that they wouldn't use such a facility even if one did exist.

Coping Patterns and Respondent Networks

Family.

Only one respondent indicated having no family. For the remaining 59 respondents, type of family member, their numbers, and residency pattern are illustrated in Table 8.

Table 8

Family Residency Patterns   n = 59

Family Member	Residency				
	Same residency	Immediate neighborhood	San Diego County	Outside San Diego	N/A
Brothers/sisters	0	4	16	23	30
Children	20	17	40	36	4
Grandchildren/ great grandchildren	5	16	27	14	22
Parents	2	4	4	1	49
Others	1	2	6	7	46

Contact with their relatives was indicated to be frequent, with two-thirds of the sample talking with or seeing their relatives on a daily basis. The majority (70 percent) reported satisfaction with their frequency of contact, 23 percent reported wanting to see them more often, but indicated distance as the deterring factor, and 2 percent wanted to see their relatives less often.

Helping patterns.

When asked to whom they turn first in time of difficulty, the majority answered, "family." When given areas of specific needs such as sickness, transportation, finances, conversation, help around the house, and food, family was again the primary source to whom the sample would turn for assistance. (See Table 9.)

Table 9
Who Helps According to Need   n = 60

Area of Need	Self/no one f	Self/no one %	Family f	Family %	Friend f	Friend %	Neighbor f	Neighbor %	Agency or Professional Person f	Agency or Professional Person %	Member, Organized Group f	Member, Organized Group %	Other f	Other %	D/K f	D/K %	N/A f	N/A %
Sickness	1	2	45	75	2	3	1	2	11	18[1]	-	-	-	-	-	-	-	-
Transportation	9	15	38	65	4	7	4	7	4	7	-	-	1	2	-	-	-	-
Financial Minor	20	33	23	38	2	3	-	-	6	10[2]	1	2	3	5	2	3	3	5
Financial Major	10	17	18	30	-	-	-	-	18	30[2]	-	-	11	18	-	-	3	5
Talking/counseling	6	10	31	52	13	23	1	2	1	2	-	-	4	7	1	2	3	5
Help around house	3	5	23	38	4	7	-	-	24	40[3]	-	-	2	3	1	2	3	5
Food	1	2	13	22	3	5	-	-	3	5	-	-	6	10	4	7	30	50*

1. Professional person = medical doctor
2. Agency = bank, credit union
3. Professional person = specific to need (e.g., plumber, appliance repairman)

* Half of the respondents did not respond to the question regarding lack of food by answering who or where they would turn to for help. Instead, half of the sample would characteristically laugh and ask what the question meant or indicate that they or "Japanese" would never be out of food.

Helping others.

Seventy-three percent of the respondents indicated that they helped friends, neighbors (45 percent), and family (17 percent). A contradiction is noted in that the respondents identified family members over friends and neighbors as persons to whom they go for help and yet indicated friends and neighbors more frequently than family as persons to whom they gave assistance. The two primary types of assistance given were talking/counseling and daily assistance, such as doing errands and household maintenance.

Affiliations and reference groups.

All but two of the respondents indicated affiliation with at least one organized group. Ethnic composition of the group and organizations were predominantly other Japanese Americans (88 percent).

Over two-thirds (68 percent) indicated membership in a church, although membership did not always indicate participation or involvement. By way of example, some interviewees indicated that they were members in name only. Of those who indicated church affiliation, the majority (63 percent) were affiliated with one of the three local Japanese American churches.

Although not asked, three-fourths of the sample volunteered the names of their medical doctors. Of this 76 percent, the majority (65 percent) named one of three Japanese American doctors practicing in San Diego. Because the sample was geographically dispersed, and the three doctors mentioned are all located in one specific area, it can be estimated that at least 65 percent of the sample go to a Japanese doctor regardless of distance to be traveled. Estimates from community workers and leaders in San Diego as to the prevalence of Japanese American older people utilizing Japanese American doctors are as high as 99 percent. (From community analysis/dissemination meeting of July 1, 1976.)

Almost two-thirds of the sample (65 percent) indicated that their friends consisted of other Japanese and 35 percent indicated having friends of various ethnic backgrounds. Table 10 represents the ethnic composition of the respondents' reference groups.

Table 10

Ethnic Composition of Reference Groups $n = 60$

Reference Group	Japanese		Mixed or non-Japanese		N/A or no affiliation*	
	f	%	f	%	f	%
Organized groups	53	88	5	8	2	3
Friends	38	63	21	35	1	2
Church*	38	63	3	5	19	32*
Medical doctor	39	65	7	11	14	23

* No affiliation with any church

Relationship to Formal Services

Of the total sample, over two-thirds (67 percent) replied that they were not familiar with existing services. One-third indicated that they were familiar with some service agencies. The type of agency with which respondents were most familiar were concerned with health and medical needs (25 percent).

With regard to the use of service agencies, one-fourth of the sample replied that they would utilize service agencies if needed and 10 percent indicated past or present use of established assistance agencies.

Aspects of Life Satisfaction

Immediate living environment.

Three-fourths of the sample responded that they considered the neighborhood in which they lived as "good"; 17 percent responded "fair"; 7 percent responded "poor"; and 1 percent replied that they didn't know. The most favorable aspects of a neighborhood were: good neighbors, safety, and quietness.

Of the 13 percent who replied that they would like to move, the following reasons were given: bad neighborhood, like to own house, and loneliness.

The context of their social circumstances.

Three-fourths of the sample replied that "things were better for Japanese Americans now than in the past." Reasons given for this perception included: (1) better housing, income level, and ease of living (29 percent); (2) less prejudice and discrimination (19 percent) with 5 percent adding that although the level of prejudice and discrimination was less it still existed; and (3) the attitude that life was better now because the early immigrants worked so hard in the past (15 percent).

Nineteen percent felt that things were worse for Japanese than before. Reasons given were that the Japanese community is losing old values and becoming too Americanized (9 percent), and society as a whole was worse now than in the past (10 percent). Five percent of the sample felt that life had not changed for the better or worse, but remained the same.

Perception of treatment as an older person.

Forty percent of the sample replied that they were being treated well as older persons with almost as many (37 percent) indicating that they were not being treated as well as they would like. The remainder of the sample either responded that they didn't consider themselves to be old (13 percent) or that they had never thought about how they were being treated (10 percent).

Opinions and Recommendations

Concept of aging.

Thirty-seven percent of the sample indicated physical and mental condition as the primary indicator of old age. Twenty-three percent designated chronological age and 15 percent referred to state of mind as determinants of when a person is considered to be old.

Why older people don't go for medical care.

In response to this question, most (37 percent) replied that they had no opinion or didn't know. Opinions that were expressed designated: (1) fear of illness (33 percent); (2) finances (27 percent); (3) language barrier (12 percent); (4) pride (10 percent); (5) old age (10 percent); and (6) transportation (6 percent), as reasons why older people don't go for medical care needed.

What can be done for older people who don't have enough income?

Three areas of responsibility were indicated by responses to this question. Thirty-five percent indicated one's self as responsible for one's financial situation. These respondents either referred to what should have been done in the past, such as having prepared for old age by saving and planning, or suggested what could be done by the individual in the present, such as working and cutting down on living expenses such as food and social activities.

The second realm of responsibility indicated was the government. Thirty-two percent recommended ways the government could assist lower income persons. These included: (1) increasing Social Security benefits (11 percent); (2) designation of "government" or welfare in general as responsible (11 percent); (3) free medical care (4 percent); (4) low cost housing (2 percent); (5) cutting down taxes (2 percent); and (6) "increased income" (2 percent).

The third area of responsibility designated was with the children of the elderly, with 3 percent responding that the children should look after their elderly parents.

Ten percent indicated no responsible party, but designated welfare as a source of income for low-income elderly. Half of these respondents replied that a person in need "should go to welfare." The other half responded that if you don't have children or savings you "can't help it and have to go to welfare."

Twenty percent of the sample replied that they "didn't know" what could be done.

What service providers should know.

The sample was asked if they could think of anything agency workers or other people providing services should know or be aware of that would help provide better services to Japanese Americans. In response to this inquiry, one-third of the sample answered that they didn't know or had no opinion. Of the responses received, knowledge about Japanese Americans was mentioned most often (43 percent). Specific knowledge mentioned included: (1) Japanese pride and subsequent reluctance to seek help, and (2) knowledge of intra-group differences such as those that exist between generations and differences between Japanese with a history in the United States and Japanese recently arrived from Japan.

Ability to speak Japanese was mentioned almost as frequently (41 percent), as an asset in providing better services. Other recommendations included the need for more outreach and being a kind person.

Who should help.

When asked who should be responsible for setting up new services or improving services, 40 percent replied that they didn't know, or gave no opinion. Thirty-two percent named Japanese individuals, organizations, themselves, their children or the Japanese American community in general as who should be responsible. Governmental responsibility was indicated by 22 percent of the sample and community-based bilingual agencies were mentioned by 3 percent of the sample.

Recommendations to younger Japanese Americans.

When asked what advice they would give to Japanese Americans younger than themselves, 84 percent of the recommendations were of a cultural nature which included: (1) action and behavior based on Japanese values (51 percent); (2) cultural activity and language (23 percent); and 3) appreciation and understanding of the historical accomplishments of Japanese in America (10 percent).

Behavioral recommendations included the concepts of: (1) *ninjo,* which stresses being courteous, polite, sympathetic to others and also has its opposite side of not being a menace to society or doing things that others would consider bad; (2) *oyakōkō,* respect for and obedience to one's parents; (3) *giri,* remembering and striving to fulfill one's obligations and responsibilities to others; (4) working hard; (5) being proud; and (6) being self-sufficient. Although the last three characteristics can be attributed to other cultures, they are part of traditional Japanese correct behavior.

Second, the respondents recommended continuance of the Japanese language and Japanese cultural activity such as traditional celebrations and ceremonies. An often mentioned example was the celebration of *oshōgatsu,* or New Year in the Japanese style.

Third, 10 percent of the respondents felt that younger Japanese should recognize and appreciate how hard the early immigrants worked, and understand that societal conditions were not always the way they are now. This recommendation was connected to their advice that younger Japanese Americans "keep up what Japanese worked for."

Ten percent of the recommendations were of a non-ethnic nature and included such advice as prepare for the future, be optimistic, and get an education. Six percent of the sample replied that they didn't know what they would recommend to younger Japanese Americans. Table 11 illustrates the response pattern of recommendations given.

Table   11

Recommendations to Younger Japanese

		f	%
1.	Cultural:		
	"Be a good Japanese" Action/Behavior ninjo, oyakōkō, giri, work hard, be proud, be self-sufficient	36	84.0
	Continue tradition and language	16	23.0
	Appreciate history of Japanese accomplishments, "keep up" good example	7	10.0
2.	Non-cultural:		
	Prepare for old age/future	2	3.0
	Be optimistic	1	1.5
	Get education	1	1.5
	Believe in God	1	1.5
	More communication	1	1.5
	Speak up at meetings	1	1.5
3.	Don't know	4	6.0

Traditional Values Taught Regarding Treatment of Elders and Mutual Assistance

Treatment of elders.

All but three respondents replied that they were taught to treat elders with respect and kindness. Most of the respondents replied in general terms without reference to specific ways or methods. *Toshiyori wo daijini,* is a phrase meaning "treat elders preciously" and was used frequently by the respondents to convey the general value of respect and kindness for elderly persons.

One-fourth of the respondents referred to the moral education learned as part of their schooling in Japan called *shushin,* as well as the *chokugo,* or the Imperial Rescript on Education issued in 1890. Both shushin and chokugo emphasized the importance of respect for elders and filial piety as duties and obligations to be upheld.

Specific ways to show kindness and respect for older people mentioned by the sample included: (1) use of formal, polite language, (2) to not call elders by their first names, and (3) to serve elders first at mealtimes.

Mutual assistance.

The sample was asked about learned values and ways Japanese "help each other during times of need." Data gathered indicated a general value of helping family, friends, neighbors, and anybody in need with whatever needed to be done. Twenty percent of the sample specifically mentioned shushin and chokugo when discussing the learned value of helping. Thirteen percent responded that they didn't remember what they were taught.

Variable Correlation

Correlation coefficients were computed on nine variables of the interview guide. Identification of variables and the extent of the association and relationship between these variables are indicated in Table 12. As can be seen from Table 12, significant correlations existed between variable 1 (age), 4 (income), 5 (education), and 6 (origin of birth).

Table 12
Correlation Coefficient Matrix of Nine Variables
$n = 60$

X	1	2	3	4	5	6	7	8	9
1	1.00	0.15	0.60	−0.57	−0.67	−0.70	0.04	0.42	−0.09
2	0.15	1.00	0.43	0.08	0.08	0.15	0.07	−0.07	0.26
3	0.06	0.43	1.00	−0.03	0.06	−0.11	0.15	−0.02	0.13
4	−0.57	0.08	−0.03	1.00	0.52	0.57	0.32	−0.38	0.18
5	−0.67	−0.08	0.06	0.52	1.00	0.65	0.17	−0.33	0.12
6	−0.70	0.15	−0.11	0.57	0.65	1.00	0.02	−0.28	0.18
7	0.40	0.07	0.15	0.32	0.17	0.02	1.00	−0.30	0.01
8	0.42	−0.01	−0.02	0.38	−0.33	−0.28	−0.30	1.00	−0.08
9	−0.09	0.26	0.13	0.18	0.12	0.18	−0.01	−0.08	1.00

Variables: X 1. Age in years
2. Years lived in San Diego County
3. Years lived in same neighborhood
4. Monthly income
5. Years of formal education
6. Origin of birth: native or foreign born
7. Sex
8. Marital status
9. Concept of oldness

Positive correlations indicated that respondents with more education had higher income levels (0.52). Respondents born in the United States had higher income levels (0.57) and more education (0.65).

Negative correlations indicated that older respondents had lower income levels (−0.57), older respondents had less education (−0.67), and Japan-born respondents were older (−0.70).

Methodological Findings

Precontact.

Besides an introductory letter that was mailed to all potential interviewers (see Chapter II on methodology), pre-interview contact was made with each interviewee by telephone. In 57 percent of the sample, the interviewer made one telephone visit in order to set the interview date. In 33 percent of the sample two telephone visits were made and in 10 percent three or more telephone contacts prior to the actual interview were made.

Fifty-three percent of the time spent for these precontacts were 15 minutes or less, 29 percent were 16-30 minutes, and 8 percent required 31 minutes or more.

/K. C. Ishizuka|

Interview.

In 60 percent of the interviews, the language used by both interviewer and interviewee was Japanese. In regard to specific ethnic self-identification used by the interviewee, the majority (76 percent) used the Japanese words: *Nihonjin,* meaning "Japanese" or *Nikkeijin,* which refers to a person of Japanese descent not living in Japan, to identify themselves and other Japanese Americans. Other identifiers used included: Japanese, 20 percent; Oriental, 3 percent; and *Kibei,* 1 percent. (See Table 13.)

Table 13
Ethnic Identifiers Used by the Sample
$n = 75$

	f	%
Nihonjin	44	59
Japanese	15	20
Nikkeijin	13	17
Oriental	2	3
Kibei	1	1

In 68 percent of the interviews, no one besides the interviewer and interviewee was present during the interview process. In 28 percent, others were present most of the time, and in 3 percent others were present part of the time. Of those interviews in which others were present, the other took part in the conversation to some degree (53 percent), a great deal (32 percent), and very little (15 percent).

The interviewers indicated that 60 percent of the sample understood the questions of the interview, 38 percent had some difficulty understanding the questions, and 2 percent had great difficulty.

Additionally, the interviewers indicated that 65 percent of the interviews conducted were friendly and close throughout, 23 percent began formally and became closer as the interview process continued, 7 percent maintained a formal distance throughout, and 2 percent were unresponsive.

The time spent in the actual interview ranged from less than an hour (2 percent) to four or more hours (13 percent). Most of the interviews (42 percent) were two to three hours long with 23 percent taking place between one and two hours, and 20 percent taking from three to four hours in length.

/K. C. Ishizuka|.

IV. ANALYSIS OF FINDINGS

The following analysis revolves around the three objectives of the study as outlined in Chapter I. These consist of: (1) the study sample's use of and perceptions toward formal assistance, (2) the relationship between the sample's characteristic lifestyle and their interaction with formal assistance agencies, and (3) the methodology used by the study.

Because of the intra-group diversity that emerged, which will be discussed in Chapter V, many of the findings and conclusions are not equally representative of all Japanese American older people.

Use and Perception of Formal Assistance Systems

The sample as a whole indicated little knowledge or use of formal service agencies. Only one-third indicated having some knowledge of their availability or existence and only 10 percent of the sample indicated ever having used service agencies.

During the debriefing sessions, the interviewers reported that the section of the interview guide regarding use and knowledge of agencies was the most difficult section for which to obtain responses. Although there were some interviewees who exhibited interest in knowing more about certain services, most were reported to be uninterested. For example, the interviewers reported that in contrast to other areas of the interview that stimulated extended and animated conversation, the area regarding formal assistance elicited (1) short answers, (2) few if any questions, and (3) little sharing of information or experiences.

Some of the respondents were perceived by the interviewers to have been uncomfortable when discussing service agencies by either becoming very quiet or reacting with emphatic statements of self-reliance and their ability to take care of themselves.

The use of formal assistance was generally said to be considered only after other sources, namely one's self and family, were exhausted. Some of the respondents used the phrase "only if destitute" to describe the circumstances under which they would seek outside assistance. Therefore, use of formal assistance is seen as a third order of coping after self and family.

Relationship Between Lifestyle and Interaction With Formal Assistance

From the research findings, it is concluded that the lifestyle of the study sample had considerable influence on the sample's perception of and interaction with formal assistance agencies. The primary basis for this lifestyle was their ethnic identity as persons of Japanese heritage and the consequences that accompany this identity.

Importance of ethnicity.

The data indicated that the sample maintained a self-identity strongly rooted in their Japanese heritage. A key indicator of the maintenance of their ethnic identity was the self-identifiers used by the sample. As reported in the findings chapter, the majority (96 percent) identified themselves as Japanese. This self-identification is further highlighted by the absence of identifiers that might reflect their American heritage or birthplace, such as "Japanese American" or "American Japanese," which would technically be a more correct designation. Another aspect of their self-identification that emphasizes their Japanese identity is the predominant use of Japanese words for this ethnicity over the English designation. Over three-fourths of the sample used the Japanese words, Nihonjin or Nikkeijin in comparison to 20 percent who used the English word Japanese.

A second key indicator of their identity as Japanese is the ethnic composition of their reference groups. As was illustrated in Table 10, the majority of the respondent's social affiliations and friends were with other Japanese Americans. For example 88 percent of the sample belonged to a Japanese American organization (such as the Meiji Kai, the Japanese senior citizens club) or to organizations whose membership was comprised primarily of other Japanese Americans (such as a local Veterans of Foreign Wars Post). Also, approximately two-thirds of the sample indicated that their friends were primarily Japanese Americans; an equal portion indicated affiliation with one of the three local Japanese American churches; and at least two-thirds of the sample utilized a Japanese American medical doctor.

A third indicator of the sample's strong ethnic identification also reveals the impact that being Japanese has on their behavioral expectations. To the open-ended question regarding the study group's recommendations to Japanese Americans younger than themselves, response patterns seemed to indicate that to be Japanese implies more than an ethnic designation, but includes a set of behavioral roles and expectations also.

As was discussed in the preceding chapter, the majority (84 percent) of the recommendations expressed were reflective of Japanese correct behavior, the importance of maintaining Japanese traditions and language, and appreciation of the history of the Japanese experience in the United States. See Table 11 for a breakdown of the response pattern given.

A few of the respondents expressed the sentiment that even Sansei (third generation Japanese in America), Yonsei (fourth generation), and subsequent generations of Japanese Americans by virtue of their Japanese heritage should be "good Japanese" by exhibiting certain behaviors and maintaining custom and language.

Impact of identity on interaction with formal assistance.

A primary consequence of the sample's strong Japanese identity in terms of interaction with formal assistance is the indication given by the sample that other Japanese can know and understand them best. With this attitude, because service providers and other agency personnel are characteristically non-Japanese, agency service providers are not apt to be sought after by Japanese American elderly in times of difficulty.

The interviewers encountered this attitude frequently throughout the interview process. For example, in response to the question of who should be responsible for setting up new services or improving services, one-third of the sample indicated other Japanese as responsible. While some of the respondents simply referred to Japanese individuals or organizations as the responsible party, others explained that Japanese should be primarily responsible because then there would be better communication and less misunderstanding.

As requisites for better communication and less misunderstandings, the respondents identified the ability to speak Japanese and also the ability to "understand Japanese people." By way of example, one respondent stated, "Japanese people know more about Japanese people, right?" Another responded, "If there were Japanese people, it would be easy to ask them questions, wouldn't it?"

Another example that highlights the attitude that Japanese can best understand other Japanese is the prominent use of Japanese American medical doctors by the study sample. As was discussed in the previous chapter, at least two-thirds of the sample go to a Japanese American medical doctor and estimates from community leaders and workers are as high as 99 percent. This is not only an illustration of the importance of ethnic identity, but also of the impact that ethnicity has on the types of assistance sought. The Japanese American doctors referred to, speak Japanese and were believed to behave in the same cultural context as their Japanese American clientele and therefore better understand their specific needs. One respondent summed up this feeling by saying, "Nihonjin wa yappari Nihonjin no docta ga ii" or "For Japanese, a Japanese doctor is best."

Coping pattern #1: Self-reliance.

When confronted with a difficulty, the sample exhibited a tendency to first rely on themselves and either (a) give themselves the assistance needed to overcome the problem or (b) adjust themselves to adapt to the difficulty. Although the sample as a whole exhibited this tendency, the degree of self-reliance declared was variant. At one end of the continuum of responses, some adamantly stated that they would "never allow themselves to be in a situation to need help from others." Others simply stated, "you have to make do with what you have."

One indicator of this value of being responsible for yourself was exhibited in the response pattern to the question regarding what can be done for older people who don't have an adequate income. Thirty-five percent indicated that individuals are responsible for their financial situation and should either rely on themselves to improve the situation, for example by working if healthy, or learn to survive on low income by making necessary alterations such as not eating as much and eliminating social activities.

Besides verbal expressions of the necessity of "making do" with what they have, another indicator of this tendency and value is implied by the prevalent response pattern of replying "don't know" or "have never thought about it" to open-ended questions. Many had no opinions on such topics as what service providers should know about Japanese Americans (33 percent) and what can be done for older people without adequate income (20 percent). Non-opinionated responses to such questions imply the focusing of energy on the empirical by the respondents and their preoccupation with the situation at hand rather than their involvement in the realm of possibilities and wishful thinking. Another possible explanation for the high incidences of such responses may be that the questions and/or mode of inquiry were not appropriate to the sample to elicit opinions and responses.

A second indicator of the tendency to be satisfied and make do with their situation was implied by (1) the sample's tendency to understate problem areas and (2) the overall modesty with which some respondents made judgments regarding aspects of their life situations. For example, in response to what was causing them the greatest difficulty, half of the sample replied that they had none, although survey responses and debriefing sessions indicated that many of those who replied that they had no problems did not, in fact, have abundant and optimal living conditions.

Another example of modesty and understating difficulties is implied by the prevalent use of neutral words to describe personal situations. For example, to describe their health, financial situations, and neighborhood, many respondents used words such as "okay," "satisfied," "normal," and "tolerable." Such neutral evalutions imply acceptance of their situation regardless of the quality and are therefore indicative of the tendency to be satisfied and "make do" with one's present situation.

The data suggested two primary reasons for this high degree of self-reliance. The first was a strong sense of personal and ethnic pride.

Two Japanese sayings told by some of the respondents in the study illustrate this sense of pride. One was the proverb, *"Bushi wa kuwanedo takayoji"* which means "although you do not have anything to eat, you use a toothpick to give the appearance of just having eaten." This saying illustrates a high degree of pride and also the hesitancy to admit or show need, even hunger. The other phrase was *"iza kamakura"* which conveys the concept of being prepared for crises.

The second explanation for the high degree of self-reliance expressed was indicated by some of the respondents' concern to not be or put a burden on others. The Japanese phrase that was often used to relate this concern was *"meiwaku o kakenai yōni,"* which translates "so as not to put a burden on another person." Therefore, it seems that for some, the motivating force behind their self-reliance is "to not put a burden on another person."

Coping pattern #2: Turn to family.

After expressing their initial tendency to rely on themselves when asked to whom it is they go when in need of various types of assistance, family members were consistently designated. Also, persons who helped were designated as living within the respondents' respective neighborhoods. Therefore, because only 3 percent of the sample lived with their adult children, a webwork of family supports geographically surrounding the respondent is indicated.

Outside assistance in the form of medical doctors, banks, credit unions, and specialized professional people such as plumbers and applicance repairmen were also utilized as can be seen from Table 10. But with the possible exception of medical doctors, these types of agencies and professional people were regarded as resources rather than as service providers. For example, the bank was not considered a service agency in that it was their own money it was keeping. Plumbers and other skilled repairmen are likewise not service providers in the social sense of the phrase because they are hired for a particular skill. Therefore, analysis of the use of these institutions and professional people conclude them to be manifestations of knowing how to help oneself by utilizations of resources rather than use of or reliance on service agencies.

Coping pattern #3: Formal assistance.

In light of the priority of self-reliance and secondarily family reliance, formal assistance is seen as a third order alternative for meeting social and personal needs.

Attitudes toward this alternative as a way of coping were expressed with a wide range of intensity. A few respondents adamantly stated that they would never go to an agency for assistance and some replied that they would go to a service agency "only if destitute." The majority perceived formal assistance as the third level of coping and would utilize an agency only when self and family lacked the adequate or necessary means to provide the help needed. A few stated that they would be willing to use an agency if and when it was needed. This three-order pattern of coping was characterized by a statement made in response to the topic of what could be done for older people without adequate income: "If you don't have savings (i.e., rely on oneself) or if you don't have children (i.e., family) you can't help it, you have to go to welfare."

Psycho-cultural price.

In searching for possible reasons for the underutilization of formal assistance agencies by the sample, the research team formulated the concept of a personal psychological price based on an internalized cultural system of values.

As mentioned, a high degree of self-pride results in the inclination to rely on oneself. As this tendency is put into practice successfully, it becomes an ability, a positive characteristic which returns to the person as a source of pride.

Figure 2
Reciprocal Nature of Self-Reliance and Pride

According to the three-order pattern of coping identified however, if agency services are utilized, self and family as resources have already been exhausted which is perceived by some as an "inability" of self and family to meet necessary needs. To the extent that self-reliance is a source of pride, not to be able to take care of oneself is therefore a source of shame. In this way it is hypothesized that if service utilization is perceived as an inability to care of self and as a source of shame, services will be underutilized.

Figure 3
Psycho-Cultural Price Resulting in
Underutilization of Services

The interviewers reported an apparent double standard that the study sample held with regard to the utilization of service agencies by Japanese and non-Japanese. This double standard is in part supportive of the concept that a high psycho-cultural price prevents unencumbered utilization of services. When discussing the realm of utilization of services, the interviewers reported that use by non-Japanese was perceived by the study sample to be of little consequence. For example, agency use by non-Japanese was said to be "okay" and did not evoke emotionally negative or positive reactions. On the other hand, the interviewers reported that utilization of services by the respondents themselves or other Japanese was seemingly evaluated by other standards.

By way of example, phraseology changed as the interviewees referred to "having to rely" on "government" or "welfare." The term "having to rely" connotes a negative perception that utilization of service is indicative of reliance or dependence rather than perceived as a right or resource. The restatement of "service agency" into "government" and "welfare," indicated that service systems were perceived of as federal and welfare agencies to the exclusion of private non-profit agencies whose purpose is to serve the public and enhance the quality of life.

Another example of a double standard is that declarative statements such as "only if destitute" and "only as a last resort" were evoked, only when discussing personal or Japanese use of service agencies. Because utilization of social services by non-Japanese was perceived to be inconsequential, social services per se were not indicated to be inherently negative. Rather, the negativity seems to result from utilization of social services by themselves as persons of Japanese heritage.

Methodological Findings

This research effort attempted to provide an honest reflection of the social reality of the study populations concerned and at the same time, to make the process of data collection a pleasant experience for the interviewee. The methodology as outlined in Chapter II was selected for its aspects that would actualize these purposes.

Community involvement.

Input and involvement from members of the Japanese American community throughout the research process proved to be a vital aspect of the project. Without the advice and cooperation of many individuals in the community, this research project could not have been conducted.

In the process of obtaining interviewers, community leaders and concerned individuals provided necessary screening and direction that resulted in the selection of interviewers most appropriate for the study sample. Interviewers were recruited and selected who exhibited the qualities that the community consultants felt were most compatible with the elders of their community. Also, individual and organizational assistance was vital in identification of older Japanese Americans from which to draw the sample.

Community persons were consulted on various aspects of the research such as how, and even whether or not the ten dollar honorarium for each interviewee should be given. This item was a delicate subject that required advice and suggestions from persons of the community involved. Because of the predominant concern for conducting the research in a manner that would be the most pleasant and enjoyable for the participants, care was taken to handle all aspects of the interview with respect for and in congruence with the constituency of the research.

This topic of a monetary gift stimulated a great amount of discussion which included whether or not money allocation would be appropriate; possible reactions of the sample, both negative and positive; alternatives of showing appreciation; and methods of making the gift acceptable. As was mentioned in the methodology chapter and after considerable discussion, it was decided to enclose the money in an envelope with a Japanese greeting card upon which was written an expression of appreciation. It was to be clearly indicated both verbally by the interviewer, and on the card, that the money was a token of appreciation from the Research Institute conducting the research, rather than a form of payment or as coming from the interviewer herself.

Another invaluable asset of the community's involvement was the brokering and communicating roles played by some individuals. Because the coordinator maintained frequent contact with many of the interested individuals acting as consultants, it was revealed that many potential interviewees had contacted these individuals to discuss their involvement prior to agreeing to participate in the study. Also, some interviewees consulted community leaders as to what to do with the honorarium they received. Because the individuals to whom they went for consultation regarding this matter were knowledgeable about the research, they were able to encourage the respondent to participate in the study and to accept the gift without reservations.

Community persons also played a meaningful role in the analysis of the study findings. Besides individual conferences, the findings were discussed at a meeting of community leaders and workers and their input has been incorporated into the foregoing analysis.

Precontact

The quality of the precontact with the potential interviewees turned out to be very important in first establishing trust and credibility and second, in setting the stage for a pleasant interview experience. As was mentioned, all of the potential interviewees were mailed an introductory and explanatory letter before telephone contact was made. From their experiences in the interview process, the interviewers concluded that this letter had been extremely helpful in setting the stage for a smooth interview by providing the interviewee information and introduction before being contacted personally.

The interviewers also reported that the most difficult aspect of the interview process was the initial personal contact. As one interviewer stated, "you have to be assertive in a Japanese way," meaning having knowledge of and experience with participating in Japanese social protocol. For example, some Japanese have a cultural tendency to decline offers of initial reaching out for reasons of politeness and modesty. An excellent example of this is found in Appendix A. The interviewers of this study were extremely skillful in being able to differentiate unwillingness to be involved from hesitation out of politeness and were thus able to either cordially accept the declination or attempt to override the prospective interviewee's hesitations by "being assertive in a Japanese way." The interviewers sometimes made three or more telephone calls before an interview was agreed to and reported that once the interviewee agreed to participate, the interview itself was friendly and smooth.

The interview as an interpersonal experience.

The actual interview proved to be an interpersonal experience that was relatively long and generally pleasant. The aspect of time was interrelated with the quality of the experience and both were connected to the three stages of interpersonal experience.

The first stage consisted of informal social conversation before the actual interview content was discussed. Through engaging in light cordial conversation, both the interviewer and interviewee were able to get to know each other and become more comfortable. The interviewers reported that most interviewees did not seem as interested in the research project itself as they were in the interviewers as persons. The interviewers found that by sharing information about themselves, such as where they were from, the spotlight was taken off the interviewee and common bases were found which facilitated the development of trust and warmth.

Because of the conversational style of interviewing adopted by the research, the pre-interview exchange flowed very smoothly into the content area of the interview purpose. In this second stage, the combination of the pre-interview exchange and the conversational approach to interviewing resulted in an atmosphere of trust wherein honest reactions and responses were encouraged. Therefore, the interviewer was able to record as much primary behavior as the interviewee chose to share.

The open atmosphere and conversational style being unrestricted by a tight interview structure also allowed for extended conversation by the interviewee. The interviewers found that various questions and content areas would stimulate further discussion and one thought would lead to others. This occurrence enabled the interviewees to impart their life experiences and wisdom and also enabled the interviewers to experience the interviewee as a total person rather than to simply collect isolated pieces of information. Another consequence of this process was that it required a substantial amount of time, often running as long as four or five hours.

After such a lengthy and interpersonal interchange, the interviewers and interviewees both sometimes found it difficult to terminate the experience and often prolonged the exchange with a third stage, that of leave-taking. During this post-interview stage, many interviewees shared their hobbies, gardens or family albums with the interviewer.

It was also during this stage that the thank-you card with the monetary expression of appreciation was given to the interviewee. The reactions to receiving this honorarium were variant. Some quickly realized that it contained money, others did not. Some opened it right away while the interviewer was still there, others waited until she had left. Some accepted the money without question, others accepted it after much explanation that it was part of the research budget and assurance that it was not from the interviewer. Some insisted that the interviewer take the money back and put it into the research project, some said that they would donate it to a church or charitable organization, and others mailed it back to the Research Institute.

The interviewers reported that the majority of their interviews seemed to be pleasant experiences for the interviewees. One indicator of a positive experience was the friendliness and cooperation the interviewee exhibited during the interview process. Many offered refreshment to the interviewer and on occasion entire meals were shared. Another example of the respondents' consideration was that card tables or TV trays to write on were often provided if the interviewer and interviewee weren't already sitting around a table.

Yet another indicator was the manner in which the leave-taking was conducted. As was mentioned, many shared their hobbies and other personal items such as family albums with the interviewer. Most walked with the interviewer to her car, said that they were glad to meet and talk with her and expressed the wish to meet again or for her to come back and visit them. One interviewee, a woman of 84 years, mailed her interviewer a gift of hand-crocheted items, a hobby she can no longer engage in due to failing eyesight. This resourceful respondent mailed the package to the university address she found on the introductory letter that was sent to all prospective interviewees. Accompanying the gift was a letter expressing how much she had enjoyed talking with the interviewer and that she would be pleased to hear from her again. "If you write to me," the respondent wrote, "please write big so I can read it."

Debriefing.

Debriefing sessions with each interviewer proved to be very important in reporting observations, impressions and conversations that provided an overall picture and feeling for the persons interviewed. A great amount of data might have gone unrecorded if the interview guides and code sheets had not been supplemented by information received during the debriefing sessions.

Besides individual debriefing sessions, periodic sessions involving all the interviewers were held throughout the data collection stage and it was during these sessions that preliminary analysis of data began.

V. Further Conclusions

Besides the conclusions regarding the three original study objectives, two other noteworthy findings emerged. One is the identification of four distinct subgroups of Japanese American older people, which reflects the changing nature of the population as a whole. The other is the patterning of data that implies a dilemma regarding the consequences of Americanization.

Intra-Group Diversity

Four distinct subgroups that exhibited diverse attitudinal, and behavioral patterns were identified within the sample. These four groups consist of: (1) Issei, original immigrants from Japan, (2) Nisei, offspring of the Issei, (3) post-World War II immigrants, and (4) Kibei, Nisei who spent part of their formative years in Japan.

The intra-group diversity among Japanese Americans has generally been thought of and described in terms of generation. From the onset of this study it was recognized that besides the Issei, a number of Nisei are also in their senior years. This distinction was controlled for in the sample by selection of an equal number from each generation. This representation was obtained by utilizing visible identifiers of the two generations, namely age-group indicating generation, and primary language indicating immigrant versus non-immigrant status.

After data collection had begun, however, the dichotomy between generations became less clear-cut. Within each generational grouping an additional subgroup was identified resulting in a more heterogenous sample than was originally controlled for. The illustration appearing as Figure 4 represents the intra-group diversity that emerged from the study.

Identification of Generation I and Generation II was based on the overt indicators of age and language. Because of the absence of visible identifiers, the subgroups within each generation, namely post-World War II immigrants within Generation I and Kibei within Generation II, emerged as distinct groups only after data was collected.

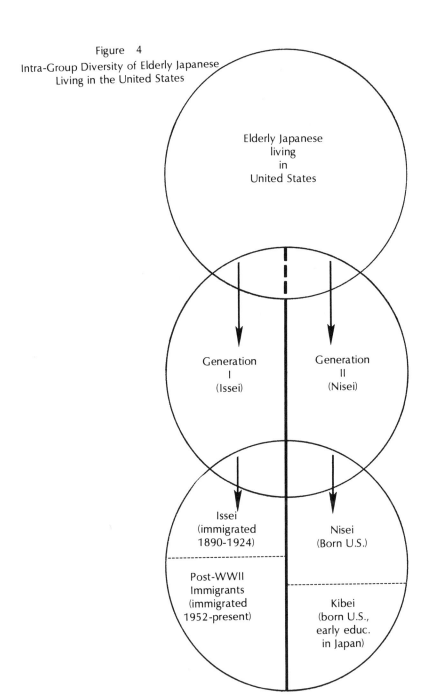

Figure 4
Intra-Group Diversity of Elderly Japanese
Living in the United States

Elderly Japanese
living
in
United States

Generation
I
(Issei)

Generation
II
(Nisei)

Issei
(immigrated
1890-1924)

Nisei
(Born U.S.)

Post-WWII
Immigrants
(immigrated
1952-present)

Kibei
(born U.S.,
early educ.
in Japan)

Once data was collected, four distinct patterns of responses emerged indicating the existence of four rather than two subgroups of Japanese American elderly. Even though the number in each of the two additional groups was small, the differences were apparent. The following brief profiles of each of the four groups highlight their distinctive characteristics. Additional information of a sociohistorical nature can be found in Appendix A.

Generation I: Issei.

The term Issei means first generation and refers to the original generation of Japanese immigrants to America. They were socialized and educated in the ways of Meiji Japan and it was the values and customs of this era of history that they brought with them as "cultural baggage" when they immigrated to America as young men and women during the late 1880s and early 1900s.

Their characteristic response pattern reflected their early teachings as indicated by the recitation of old proverbs, reference to chokugo and shushin, which were part of their formal education and also their adherence to traditional values such as obligation and self-responsibility.

Their experience as immigrants in a foreign country was also reflected in their response pattern. For example, their experience of surviving hardship and overt discrimination was manifested in a stubborn sense of self-reliance and strong distaste for outside assistance systems. Also, most Issei verbally expressed and recognized the significance of their pioneer days of hardwork and perseverance.

Generation I: Post-World War II immigrants.

This subgroup of elderly Japanese Americans remained in Japan while their Issei immigrant counterparts immigrated to America. There in Japan, they were a part of the modernization and Westernization of Japan. With this background they immigrated to America a half century later with a different set of "cultural baggage" than did the Issei.

In comparison to the response pattern of the Issei, these elderly of more recent immigration, did not reflect the ways and customs of old Japan. For example, while the Issei frequently referred to chokugo and shushin and emphasized the impact it had and continues to have on their lives, these concepts were rarely, if ever, mentioned by the more recent immigrants.

Also, post-World War II immigrants did not exhibit the intensity of self-reliance and unwillingness to utilize outside assistance that the Issei expressed. Having been a part of Japan's social changes, which included the increased availability of services, they had the experience of having sanctioned access to service systems within a Japanese structure which the Issei did not. A further difference in their response pattern was the absence of referring to a pioneer life in America.

Generation II: Nisei.

Children of the Issei are called Nisei or second generation Japanese in America. Now entering their later years, the Nisei were raised in the United States in Japanese fashion by their Japanese parents. However, most Nisei have had little direct experience with the land of their ethnic heritage. While most have visited

Japan as children and adults, Nisei have spent the majority of their years in the United States.

Their response pattern was indicative of their dual heritage and represented a mix of Japanese and American behaviors and attitudes. For example, the Nisei's Japanese heritage was reflected in their learning of traditional values such as filial piety and treating elders with kindness and respect, being able to speak or understand Japanese and identification of themselves as Japanese.

Their American heritage, in contrast to Generation I, was reflected in their greater involvement with the American society at large. For example, they were educated in the United States, engaged in a wider range of activities, and had more affiliations outside the Japanese community than did the Issei.

Generation II: Kibei.

Kibei are Nisei who were sent to Japan during their childhood to receive a Japanese education and socialization. They returned to the United States as teenagers who had developed a set of experiences, expectations and behaviors different from those of their Nisei brothers and sisters who remained in America.

In contrast to the Nisei who were familiar with the Japanese language, but whose primary language was English, most Kibei of the sample were more comfortable in Japanese. Having direct experience with pre-World War II Japan, they learned chokugo and shushin which the Nisei did not and like the Issei referred to them frequently.

Many of the Kibei respondents expressed feeling somewhat estranged from the Nisei and also expressed closeness of identification with and feeling for the Issei.

Changing profile of the population.

As manifested by the emergence of the four subgroups, the population of Japanese American older people is currently undergoing a state of change. This alteration of character is due to the recent transition of the Nisei / Kibei generation into the age category of elderly and the recent immigration of elderly from Japan.

As yet, very little is known about the ways these changes impact on the population from a social gerontological perspective. The identification of the intra-group diversity among Japanese American older people is a particularly meaningful finding in terms of future research, the advancement of knowledge and improvement of service delivery systems.

Dilemma of Americanization

The second noteworthy finding is that the data indicated a dilemma regarding the process of Americanization. As expressed by the study sample, the impact of Americanization was felt to have both positive and negative consequences.

Positive consequences of Americanization.

Americanization was viewed as positive by the study sample in that advanced technology and modernization in conjunction with less overt discrimination and greater opportunities have made life physically more comfortable for them. For example, in response to whether life for Japanese Americans is presently better, same, or worse, the majority of the sample replied that the situation as a whole was better now in contrast to the past. Primarily, life was perceived to be better now because physical and material life needs were being met: housing was better, income was higher, and opportunities were greater.

Negative consequences of Americanization.

Americanization was also perceived as being negative by the study sample. It was expressed that Japanese Americans were becoming "too Americanized" in attitude and behavior, thereby forsaking old values and behavioral standards. In this context, Americanization was thought to cause a breakdown of traditional family and community mutual assistance as expressed in the sentiment that "Japanese don't help each other" in contrast to the past.

In response to the question of how Japanese help each other now, almost half (53 percent) of the sample stated that "Japanese don't help each other anymore." Although the data indicated that assistance and support are still available within the Japanese American community, it is theorized that in contrast to the quality and quantity of mutual assistance given and received in the past, such support was perceived to be nonexistent by almost half of the entire sample. It also may be that the kind of assistance given now may be less visible, thereby giving rise to the perception that "Japanese don't help each other anymore."

Regardless of theoretical explanations, the perception of loss of mutual assistance was expressed with much remorse and cannot be denied. It represents a manifestation of the dilemma of Americanization and reflects a real perceived loss.

In conclusion, the respondents frequently referred to the old Japanese ways which have been diluted by the process of Americanization. On a material and physical level, life was perceived to be better now than in the past. However, on a more personal level, the perceived breakdown of the "old ways" was felt with sadness by many of the respondents.

One consequence of the negative perception of Americanization may be upon the quality of life satisfaction as older people. For example, over one-third (37 percent) of the respondents replied that they were not being treated as well as they would like. This is only two respondents less than the number who indicated that they were being treated well, the rest having expressed no opinions. Those who were not satisfied with the way they were being treated often highlighted the contrast between cultural values of the present and the past. One respondent captured this feeling by saying, "As a young person, I was taught the old way of respect for older people. Now that I am older myself, I realize how nice the old ways were."

VI. Recommendations and Implications

Besides the findings and conclusions reported, this research project had many important and interesting recommendations and implications for areas of future research and the planning and delivery of social services.

Recommendations For Further Research

An important finding of this study that has many implications for further research is the intra-group diversity and changing nature of the population of Japanese American elderly in general. As was mentioned, the subgroups of post-World War II immigrants and Kibei emerged as distinctive groups not because of their numbers, but because of their qualitative differences. With further research, these differences could be more finely identified and quantified. Analysis and comparison could be conducted and characteristic profiles made on each subgroup. With such new and distinguishing information, specific recommendations for planning and delivery of appropriate services could be made.

An assessment of the changing nature of the population would provide greater understanding of the dynamics in progress that impact on the population of Japanese American elderly as a whole. The generation of Nisei is presently undergoing a crucial transition into their retirement years. Because their experience and lifestyles are distinct from the Issei, the characteristics of the population of elderly Japanese Americans will alter as the number of Nisei entering their senior years increases.

Another internal variable that alters the population profile is the increasing number of elderly Japanese recently arrived from Japan. As was mentioned, these elderly persons bring an entirely new dimension into the gerontological state of Japanese American elderly. Knowledge of how this group has and will impact on the future needs and concerns of the population would be beneficial and have far-reaching implications.

Another recommended area of future research would be to further explore the possible factors resulting in the underutilization of service agencies. For example, testing of the psycho-cultural price hypothesized in this paper must be conducted before it can be concluded to be a reason for agency underutilization by Japanese American elderly. More importantly, the level of appropriateness of service agencies vis-a-vis Japanese American older people and the capacity of service agencies for effectively meeting consumer needs should be scrutinized rather than assumed. Factors resulting in underutilization of services may be intrinsic to the organization and dynamic system of the agencies themselves. While there have been studies which have addressed inherent barriers to service delivery (Gilbert, 1972; Miranda and Kitano, 1976), further research of the suitability and effectiveness of service delivery systems might shed considerable light on the area of underutilization of service agencies by Japanese American older people.

Recommendations for Social Service Systems

The study sample was asked their opinion of what agencies or service providers should know in order to provide better services to Japanese Americans. Of the opinions expressed, knowledge and understanding of Japanese Americans and the ability to speak Japanese emerged as being the two most important qualities of successful service delivery.

Cultural knowledge.

The research highlighted three cultural characteristics as key concepts for the better understanding of Japanese American elderly. These characteristics are important to consider and incorporate in the planning and delivery of social services.

Strong Japanese identity.   As was discussed, the sample reflected an identity that was firmly rooted in their Japanese heritage and which had considerable impact on their lifestyle, coping patterns and interaction with formal assistance. Awareness of the importance of their ethnic identity and the impact it has on their lives as reported in this monograph is important in creating appropriate and acceptable service systems.

Because of the significance of this characteristic, implications for service delivery are many. They include the need for: (1) bicultural and bilingual staff, (2) staff training that includes an overview of cultural background and historical experiences, and (3) community involvement.

Intra-group diversity.   The sample's Japanese identity and distinctive Japanese American lifestyle were expressed in a variety of ways. Recognition of the heterogenous nature of the population of Japanese American older people is crucial for optimal service delivery. Age-group and language are major variables that are easily distinguishable and have important implications for service delivery such as the need for bilingual staff and consideration of different generations of age cohorts. As previously mentioned, these variables are also basic indicators for distinguishing between generations which is very important and yet relatively easy to do. Within generations, cultural differences interact to produce still more variety.

With awareness of this intra-group heterogeneity, caution can be exercised against the indiscriminate use of relating to Japan or things Japanese as a means of establishing trust and exhibiting cultural knowledge. While one elderly Japanese American may appreciate being told that the service provider has visited Japan and enjoyed its hospitality, another may feel that the service provider is making fun, relating stereotypically, or establishing an exotic distance between them.

Beyond the major variables of history, culture, language, and generation, the uniqueness of the personality and personal experience necessitate respect for the individual within their cultural context.

Pride.   As was mentioned, the strong sense of personal and ethnic pride exhibited by the study sample exerted a great influence on their attitude toward assistance in general and specifically on their underutilization of service agencies.

A strong sense of pride produces a tendency for self-reliance and feeling responsible for personal situations. This, in turn, results in a hesitancy to admit need or reach out for assistance.

Linguistic ability.

The ability to speak the same language was an important and crucial aspect of communication for the sample. Over half of the respondents indicated Japanese as their primary language and it was one of the two qualities of successful service delivery as expressed by the sample.

Implications for service delivery includes not only bilingual staff, but also translations of informational brochures and outreach flyers.

Implications For Service Delivery Systems

From the above recommendations, the following implications for planning and delivering services are indicated.

Community involvement.

The sample's strong ethnic identity and extensive affiliation with other Japanese Americans emphasizes the need for community involvement in all phases and aspects of planning, delivery, and evaluation of services. Beyond traditional use of community on advisory boards, community persons should be utilized in such capacities as brokering, training, consultation, and evaluation.

Outreach.

More effective methods of outreach would facilitate familiarization and ultimately utilization of social services. Because of the Japanese American elderly's hesitancy to admit need and accept services, personal contact by sensitive service providers might open what were previously thought to be closed doors.

Written outreach translated into Japanese and announcements in the Japanese American media would reach people who do not have linguistic access to public information available in English.

Bilingual and bicultural staff.

The research results indicate a need for staff persons who can speak Japanese as well as staff persons of Japanese ancestry. As was mentioned, the two identified aspects of better communication consisted of the ability to speak the same language and the indication that Japanese people can best understand other Japanese. Qualified bilingual and bicultural people are needed, not only in direct service positions, but in administrative capabilities as well.

Training.

The study highlighted the impact and importance of the sample's cultural and historical experiences. Therefore, staff training that includes some education regarding the Japanese Americans' historical and cultural roots would result in greater knowledge of and sensitivity to Japanese American clientele and prospective consumers.

Without some background and contemporary knowledge of Japanese Americans, service delivery systems may operate under such falsely assumed stereotypes as "Japanese don't need services." With underlying assumptions such as these, little attempt is made to reach out to Japanese Americans or plan appropriate services.

Recommendations For Direct Practice

Besides the above recommendations and implications for social service systems, a great deal of practical information on how to work with Japanese American older people was indicated. The methods of interviewing are similar to that of providing direct service, in that there is personal one-to-one contact with the respondent/client, as well as an exchange of human interaction and specific information that takes place. Indeed, the interviewers of this study delivered many services in the form of information and referral, and in some situations, acted as advocates and sources of transportation.

Beyond the recommendations of a cultural nature, when discussing qualities of optimal service delivery, the sample also indicated a personal quality unrelated to cultural consideration; that a service provider should be *shinsetsu na hito* or a "kind person." From the research findings, the following qualities of what makes a kind person are implied.

A service provider would be a kind person if he or she is: (1) aware and sensitive to the hesitation and uncomfortableness which the Japanese American elder experiences when utilizing services, and (2) is able to operationalize this sensitivity by attempting to deliver needed services without engendering a loss of self-respect or dignity. In other words, the service provider must reduce the psycho-cultural price of the Japanese American elder who is in need of services. To realize this purpose, the service provider begins by establishing credibility and gaining trust.

The interviewers concluded that the quality of their initial contact with the interviewee was crucial in actualizing these goals. In both the telephone contact before their meeting and the informal conversation engaged in prior to the interview itself, the interviewers identified certain behavioral qualities that helped create an atmosphere of trust which when maintained, resulted in a pleasant and successful interview. The following recommendations for direct practice are based on the interviewers' experience and success in establishing and maintaining trust.

Be patient. Don't insist on direct answers or expect instant rapport. Direct the conversation according to the task at hand with sincere interest in and concern for the consumer.

Be open. Exchange greetings, establish commonalities by sharing information about yourself and honestly explain your purpose in a straightforward and friendly manner. The interviewers found that by being open and sharing information about themselves, the respondents not only came to trust them but reciprocated by also being honest and sincere.

Show interest. Show sincere interest in the person to whom you are talking. By being observant and attentive, sensitive service providers can learn a lot about their clients.

Implications.

The implications of these recommendations for successful service delivery emphasize adequate time-budget allocation for interpersonal exchange and the ability and willingness of the service provider to reach out and make meaningful connection with the client.

Cost effectiveness of service delivery must be evaluated in terms of quality and outcome of interaction rather than strictly by numerical accounting procedures. Besides the qualities of cultural and linguistic capabilities, service providers should be selected and trained according to the three previously identified personal qualities of a kind person.

GLOSSARY OF COMMONLY USED TERMS*

Words

Issei:	first generation (Japanese in America)
Nisei:	second generation (Japanese in America)
Kibei:	Nisei with early Japanese education
Sansei:	third generation (Japanese in America)
Yonsei:	fourth generation (Japanese in America)
Nihonjin:	Japanese person(s)
Nikkeijin:	person(s) of Japanese ancestry living outside of Japan as the citizen of a country other than Japan
Kokujin:	Black person(s)
Hakujin:	Caucasian person(s)
toshiyori:	older person(s); an aged person(s)
Bushido:	Code of the Samurai (Warrior)
Kyōiju-chokugo:	Imperial Rescript on Education, proclaimed by Emperor Meiji on October 20, 1890.
enryo:	reserve, reservation, restraint, diffidence
gaman:	patience and perseverance, self-command, forbearance
giri:	moral obligation to others
haji:	shame, humiliation
kimi ni chugi:	loyalty to Emperor
chū-kō:	loyalty to Emperor and filial piety to parents
on:	psychological indebtedness that obligates an individual to pay back by showing loyalty and doing service to benefactor whose act has created such "indebtedness."
oyakōkō:	filial piety to parents
shinbo:	like gaman, perseverance in adversity, endurance, patience
shūshin:	moral education taught in Japan before World War II (meaning "self-control")
koden:	gift of money given to family of deceased at the funeral (meaning "incense money"); an obituary gift
oshōgatsu:	New Year's Day Celebration
sabetsu:	discrimination
shashin kekkon:	picture marriage (a man and a woman by only seeing each other's photographs, agree to marry)
yasashiku:	tenderly and affectionately; in response to how elderly should be treated

/K. C. Ishizuka|

Phrases

danketsu shiteinai:	lacking a group solidarity
kimochi ga warui:	"doesn't feel right"
meiwaku o kakenai yoni:	"So as not to put a burden on another person," in order not to bother others
Nihon no bitoku:	virtues of Japan
Nihonjin no hokori:	pride of the Japanese
shikata ga nai:	"It can't be helped," implying to make do with what you have—there is nothing to be done about it.
shima guni konjō:	small island spirit: an insularism
shinsetsu na hito:	kind person(s)
toshiyori o daijini:	treat elders with kindness and respect
yamato damashii:	Japanese spirit

Proverbs

Bushi wa kuwanedo takayōji:	Although you do not have anything to eat, you use a toothpick to give the appearance of just having eaten and being satisfied.
Iza Kamakura:	concept of being prepared for emergency or crisis
Mago wa koyori kawaii; or Jibun no koyori mago no hōga kawaii:	Grandchildren are more dear than one's own children.
Monzen no kozō narawanu kyo o yomu:	"Boys in front of the temple gate chant sutras untaught." By hearing, even without listening, over and over again the same song of sutra, we shall, especially if young, soon learn it by heart without any effort to do so. (Okada, 1960)
Ninomiya Sontoku:	a greatly admired man who was held up as a model and inspiration for correct behavior in Japan. Taking care of elderly parents was one of his virtues.
Oyano iken to nasubi no hana wa sen ni hitotsu mo ada ga nai:	A parent's advice, like the flower of the eggplant, fails not even once in a thousand.

There are five vowels (a, i, u, e, o) in Japanese and they are pronounced briefly like in Spanish: "a" like u in "summing up"; "i" like i in "pit"; "u" like u in "put"; "e" like e in "pet"; and "o" like o in "ox". However, they are also pronounced in a long way and in the romanization of the words, "−" is placed on top of each of them: a, i, u, e, o are pronounced like "ah", "ee", "oo" (woo), "eh", "oh". (H.W.)

* Grateful acknowledgment is extended to Professor Hiroshi Wagatsuma of the Department of Anthropology at the University of California, Los Angeles for translation of the following terms.

METHODOLOGICAL REFERENCES

Alvarez, Rudolfo.   The unique psychohistorical experience of the Mexican American people. *Social Science Quarterly,* 1971, *52* (1), 12-29.

Blauner, Robert, & Wellman, David.   Toward the decolonization of social research. In Joyce A. Laher (Ed.) *The death of white sociology.* New York: Vintage Books, 1973.

Campbell, Donald T., & Stanley, Julian.   *Experimental and quasi experimental designs for research.* Chicago: Rand McNally College Publishing Co., 1963.

Clark, Margaret, & Anderson, Barbara Gallatin.   *Culture and aging: An anthropological study of the older American.* Springfield, Ill.: Charles C. Thomas, 1967.

Cooley, Charles H.   Primary groups. In Paul H. Hare, Edgar F. Borgutta, & Robert F. Bales (Eds.) *Small groups: Studies in social interaction.* New York: Alfred A. Knopf, 1955.

Counting the forgotten: The 1970 census count of persons of Spanish-speaking background in the United States. Washington, D.C.: U.S. Government Printing Office, 1974.

Federal Register. Title 45: public welfare, Part 46: protection of human subjects, 1975, *40* (50), 11854-11858.

García, Ernest.   Chicano Spanish dialects and education. *Aztlan,* 1971, *2* (1), 67-73.

Glaser, Barney G., & Straus, Anselom L.   *The discovery of grounded theory.* Chicago: Aldine Publishing Co., 1967.

Gouldner, Alvin (Ed.).   Explorations in applied social science. In Alvin W. Gouldner, & S.M. Miller (Eds.) *Applied sociology opportunities and problems.* New York: The Free Press, 1965.

Hamilton, Charles.   Black social scientists: Contributions and problems. In Joyce Ladner (Ed.) *The death of white sociology.* New York: Vintage Books, 1973.

Lofland, John.   *Analyzing social settings.* Belmont, Pennsylvania: Wadsworth Publishing Co., Inc., 1974.

Moore, Joan W.   Situational factors affecting minority aging. *Gerontologist,* 1971, *2* (2), 88-93.

—————————. Social constraints on sociological knowledge: academics and research concerning minorities. *Social Problems,* 1973, *21* (1), 65-77.

Murase, Kenji.   Ethnic minority content in the social work curriculum: Social welfare policy and social research. In *Perspectives on ethnic minority content in social work education.* Boulder, Colo.: Western Interstate Commission for Higher Education, 1972.

Romano, Octavio.   The historical and intellectual presence of Mexican Americans. *El Grito,* 1969, *2* (2), 13-26.

Sieber, Sam D.   The integration of field work and survey methods. *American Journal of Sociology,* 1973, *48,* 1335-1359.

Solomon, Barbara.   Growing old in the ethnosystem. In E. Percil Stanford (Ed.) *Minority aging: Proceedings of the Institute on Minority Aging.* San Diego: The Campanile Press, San Diego State University, 1974.

Stebbins, Robert A.   The unstructured research interview as interpersonal relationship. *Sociology and Social Research*, 1972, 56, 164-179.

Takagi, Paul.   The myth of "assimilation in American life." *Amerasia Journal*, 1973, 2, 149-158.

Truzzi, Marcello (Ed.).   *Verstehen, subjective understanding in the social sciences.* Reading, Mass.: Addison, Wesley Publishing Co., 1974.

Vaca, Nick C.   The Mexican American in the social sciences, 1912-1970, part I. *El Grito*, 1970, 7 (1), 53-78.

——————— The Mexican American in the social sciences, 1912-1970, part II. *El Grito*, 1970, 3 (3), 3-24.

Valle, Ramón.   *Amistad-compadrazgo as an indigenous webwork, compared with the urban mental health network.* Unpublished doctoral dissertation, University of Southern California, 1974.

Webb, Eugene; Campbell Donald; Schwartz, Richard; & Schrest, Lee.   *Unobstrusive measures: Non-reactive research in the social sciences.* Chicago: Rand-McNally Co., 1971.

APPENDIX A
HISTORICAL AND CULTURAL OVERVIEW
OF JAPANESE AMERICAN ELDERLY

Intimate knowledge of and full sensitivity to the historical predicament and cultural patterns of Asian Americans is necessary for effective treatment and successful delivery of services (Hatanaka, Watanabe & Ono, 1975). The following includes a sociohistorical overview of the Japanese experience in America and a summary of cultural patterns and characteristics.

Sociohistorical Overview

Besides living their lives as unique beings who experience universal joys and sorrows as well as the many responsibilities of daily life, older people are examples of living history. Japanese American older people share a certain history, each with his/ her own reactions, feelings, and circumstances. The following is a brief summary of historical circumstances through the knowledge of which we may gain a fuller understanding of Japanese American older people.

Cultural dissonance.

The Issei were socialized in an agrarian, family-centered culture of rural Meiji Japan which included a collective orientation with well defined roles and rules for behavior. As residents of the United States, however, they are now growing old in a foreign country and contemporary society that is characterized by transitory, unstable families and independent lifestyles that defy prescription of roles or circumscription to rules. The Issei, therefore, find themselves in an atmosphere and environment at apparent odds with their beginnings. (Kalish and Moriwai, 1973)

Although growing old in any society involves some age-related losses, Issei must also deal with a cultural discrepancy in the way elders of the society are treated. Japanese American elderly grew up in an environment where the tradition and expectation was that elders, by virtue of their advanced years, have earned and are due added respect and certain privileges not bestowed upon the young or middle aged. Whether this heightened status would have been experienced by the Issei had they remained in Japan is not the issue here. Rather, what we must acknowledge is that in general, Japanese American older people were taught that the elderly were to be treated with respect, and that they grew up with the expectation that they would be treated likewise in their later years. This orientation and expectation has not been realized in their old age in America where the emphasis is on youth, productivity, and progress.

Caudill (1952), Iga (1966), and Kitano (1969) have commented that such Japanese characteristics as politeness, diligence, and thrift are congruent with American middle-class values and therefore have facilitated rather than hindered the Japanese American adjustment to American life. Kalish and Moriwaki (1973) point out, however, that these qualities are motivated by cultural values such as: (1) dependence of the individual on the family group, (2) obedience to Emperor and elders, and (3) rules for proper behavior. Such value systems are not supported or manifested in contemporary American life. Although, on the surface, Japanese Americans seem to fit into the social structure of American middle class, their maintenance of a lifestyle firmly rooted in Japanese norms and values provided a cultural dissonance in the social reality of the Japanese American.

History of legalized discrimination.

Japanese emigration to America began during the late 1800s and early 1900s. They came to the West Coast as laborers in hopes of making their fortunes and returning to their homeland. Not only did they find that economic success was not easily attainable, they found that physical survival, rather than financial success, became the primary goal. When they arrived, the West Coast already had a history of thirty years of anti-"Oriental" sentiment and with their arrival, this sentiment quickly became legalized by law and intensified in emotional attitude, as well as manifested in overt acts of violence.

As "aliens ineligible for citizenship" until 1952, the Issei were subjected to numerous acts of codified discrimination. The first was the so-called "Gentlemen's Agreement" in 1908 under which the Japanese government agreed to stop the emigration of Japanese laborers to the United States.

In 1913, California passed the Webb Act, an alien land law, which prohibited Japanese from buying or leasing land for more than three years. This law was amended in 1920 to forbid Issei from buying land in the names of their Nisei children who were United States citizens by birth (JACL, 1975).

The United States Congress passed the Cable Act in 1922, an antimiscegenation law, which provided that "any woman who marries an alien ineligible for citizenship (i.e., Japanese) shall cease to be an American citizen" (JACL, 1975).

In 1924, the Immigration Exclusion Act halted all immigration to the United States from Japan. After World War II in 1952, the Walter-McCarran Act was passed which extended token immigration quotas to Asian nations and the right of naturalization to the Issei. (JACL, 1975.)

In 1965, passage of a new immigration bill eliminated race, creed, and nationality as bases for immigration and immigration from Japan resumed. Because of these historical acts, Japanese immigration occurred during two distinct periods. The first took place between 1890 and 1924. The second period of immigration began after 1952 and continued to the present. Table A represents the time sequence of Japanese immigration.

Table A
Total Japanese Immigration

1890-1900	27,440
1901-1910	132,706
1911-1920	87,576
1921-1930	39,237
1931-1940	-0-
1941-1950	-0-
1951-1960	46,250
1961-1970	38,500

SOURCE: *The Experience of Japanese Americans in the United States,* JACL, 1975 and *A Study of Selected Socio-Economic Characteristics of Ethnic Minorities Based on the 1970 Census, Volume II: Asian Americans,* Office of Special Concerns, Department of Health, Education and Welfare, 1974.

In 1942 President Franklin Roosevelt signed Executive Order 9066 which authorized the removal of all Japanese aliens and "non-aliens" (i.e., U.S. citizens) from designated areas of the West Coast, resulting in the mass relocation and internment of 112,000 persons of Japanese heritage, two-thirds of whom were United States citizens by birth. However, as Gee (1971) reminded, although the oppressive legal sanctions that confronted the Issei were a reality and part of their shared history, it must be remembered that they are not a nameless mass victimized by history, but rather active human participants in the making of history. Rather than just asking what was done to the Issei, we should examine the human drama in their history for the sources of the tremendous strength of character which enabled them to survive racial injustice, poverty, hardwork, and loneliness with dignity and honor.

Impact of World War II internment.

Effects of incarceration are far reaching and unique to the individual. Its impact on the aging process of the middle aged as the Issei were and the teen aged as older Nisei were, is profound and variant.

The Issei were in their 40s and 50s when they were uprooted and placed in what were called "relocation camps"—violently disassociated from the fruits of their most productive years. Being "aliens ineligible for citizenship," they were politically powerless to protect their families from incarceration or from losing their life possessions and savings.

The following excerpt from a journal written by an Issei man during his incarceration reveals an example of the psychological and external states of confusion and insecurity.

This action is against American Constitution—a black spot for Democracy, but Army paid no attention. I educated my daughters to be best citizen of U.S.A. and America is my resting place after I am deceased. Alas, the daughters—typical American citizens—must face music as Issei.

We are now facing most disturbing and catastrophic situation, and have not any solution. The West Coast Commander issued the most merciless and ruthless one in all my life. Moving day was the most lamentable and sorrowful day in all our life—our foundation, built by fifty years of hard toil, was swept away by Army's Order. It was awful nightmare!

If peace will be restored in some future, I won't have any money left. This problem worries me days and nights, but I don't have any idea for solution. (Bosworth, 1967.)

Besides being stripped of their possessions, Japanese Americans experienced hardship in their personal and family lives. Families were often physically separated, meals were served army style in mess halls, lines formed for public latrines and privacy was a rare luxury. With these indignities, the Issei emerged aged beyond the two to four years they spent behind barbed wire, their dominant role as elders undermined.

The Nisei, in their teens and early twenties, not only had their uncertain futures ahead of them, but were also forced to quickly mature out of necessity and assume more responsibility than is usually expected of youth. They were often called upon as spokesmen and decision makers, for they at least had United States citizenship, spoke English, and had knowledge of American ways—for after all, they were Americans.

This fact turned out to be the Nisei's most effective tool, the only avenue open to them to expose the injustness of their internment. In order to prove that they were wrongly incarcerated, they had to prove their innocence, which meant to demonstrate their "American-ness"; for the "crime" for which they were punished was nothing but their Japanese heritage. Many felt that if they could demonstrate that they were loyal Americans, this would invalidate the false rationale for internment and thus "avenge" this insulting fact.

The forces of their internalized Japanese attitudes and the pressure they felt to be "American" have worked to both strengthen and oppress the Nisei in many ways. The Horatio Alger success story of the Japanese American reveals the success at which the Nisei have proved themselves, but the personal sacrifice has been great.

Importance of the Japanese American community.

Historically, the Japanese American community has been vital to the survival of the Japanese in the United States. The oppressive conditions the Japanese immigrants encountered strengthened the immigrants' cultural value of group behavior and the creation and maintenance of Japanese American communities became sanctuaries for physical safety, economic survival, and personal self-esteem. The ethnic community became the social structure that provided opportunities for leadership and self-actualization. As opposed to the hostile majority society, the ethnic community system provided a different set of cues and reinforcements (Miyamoto, 1972).

Miyamoto (1939) emphasized the importance of the Japanese American community by offering the community as a reason for the Japanese American's apparent success in American life. He suggested that the status achievement of Japanese Americans in Seattle, Washington was due to the high degree of community organization which the Japanese American community established, the opportunity for advancement this organization created, and the controls over the population the community exerted.

Cultural Patterns and Characteristics

"Inside" vs. "outside" perspectives.

The concept of cultural relativism proposes the notion that each culture has its own values and standards which cannot be judged by the values and standards of another culture. Because many values are culturally determined, perspectives from inside the cultural group are often very different from what is seemingly so from the outside.

For example, the Japanese concern for politeness should not be misinterpreted as weakness. The "quietness" attributed to the Japanese American is true in that to be loud and boisterous is to be rude and bothersome. This quality, however, has been misinterpreted and exploited by the majority society and requires analysis from a Japanese perspective.

As Japanese Americans are considered "quiet," they are often misinterpreted as being "non-assertive" and "passive" because they tend not to exhibit qualities of "aggression" and "verbosity" which often characterize "assertion" from a non-Japanese perspective. The "quietness" of Japanese Americans has also been called a "positive" stereotype and as such has wrongly been used as a tool of "racist love" (Chin et al., 1974) by holding the "quiet Japanese" up as a "model minority" (Nishio, 1969) for other non-white groups to follow. Such a paternalistic and exploitive attitude is an insult to Japanese Americans and other non-white groups. At the same time, this incorrect comparison provides the illusion that Japanese Americans are fully accepted and assimilated into American society. (Okimoto, 1971.)

The "quietness" attributed to Japanese Americans as a definitive characteristic of their personality is also, in part, a reaction to racism. To be inconspicuous is one way to avoid racist attacks, to survive. Japanese American older people are not quiet within their own cultural environment, but very expressive and articulate. When interacting with "outsiders" however, secondary behavior is often characterized by learned survival reactions such as being quiet.

Japanese personality and character.

As mentioned before, although not identical with Japanese from Japan, the Japanese American lifestyle is rooted in traditional Japanese culture. Therefore, explication of some common themes of traditional Japanese personality and character assists in understanding some of the characteristics of Japanese American older people as exhibited by the sample.

Caudill (1973) in a review of the literature on the Japanese personality and character, abstracted the main themes that characterize the Japanese personality. The following abstractions of traditional Japanese values and characteristics reflect many of the research findings regarding the maintenance of ethnic lifestyle by Japanese Americans, as well as provide a cultural context in which they can better understand. The degree with which Japanese American older people exhibit these traditional Japanese values is greatly affected by their generation and ties with Japan.

1. *The value of the group or community as being of central importance.* As previously mentioned, for the Issei this cultural collective orientation was doubly reinforced. First, the Issei in general, were from the poor rural areas of Japan in which subordination of individual needs and desires in favor of the family's well-being was necessary for economic survival. Second, upon immigrating to a hostile, foreign country, maintenance of group solidarity became a principal mode of survival and provided the immigrants with a social and economic arena in which to live.

2. *A strong sense of "we" vs. "they."* This theme is prevalent among Japanese Americans besides Japanese, both in terms of the distinction between "we" Japanese and non-Japanese, as well as between subgroups within the Japanese American community. In the study, the distinction between Japanese and non-Japanese was indicated by the apparent double standard which was applied to the two groups with regard to the utilization of service agencies. A distinction between Japanese and non-Japanese was also implied by the expressed sentiment that Japanese can best understand other Japanese. Within the Japanese American community, identification according to subgroup was made, with one subgroup often feeling that the other subgroups don't understand them.

3. *A strong sense of obligation and gratitude.* This concept forms the motivational basis for the naturalistic coping pattern of self and mutual assistance taught to and manifested by the study sample. Given a strong sense of obligation and gratitude, the pattern of giving assistance to anyone in need becomes a manifestation of correct living and an underlying assumption of daily life. Caudill (1952) felt that this complex system of obligation was necessary to be familiar with before the Issei and Nisei in America could begin to be understood. He also helps explain the perception, as voiced by a portion of the study sample, that Japanese don't help each other now. Attempting to act out a strong internal sense of obligation, duty, and responsibility in a society that does not provide the opportunity or supportive structures to do so is difficult. Societal conditions in which Japanese American older people presently live do not facilitate the behavioral manifestations of the value of obligation. Hence, although the sense of obligation is maintained by older Japanese Americans, the perception arises that Japanese don't help each other anymore.

4. *A willingness to work hard and to persevere.* For the Issei, Caudill (1952) felt that the major value and adaptive mechanism in the area of goals, life tasks and self-attitudes was to personally strive for success in the face of whatever odds. Even if one is tired and puzzled, and the outer world conditions imply defeat, one must nevertheless keep on and never give up. This is a manifestation of the "Japanese spirit," *Yamato Damashi,* and an important characteristic of correct Japanese conduct.

5. *An attitude of deference and politeness.* This theme was most evident in the interchange that occurred between interviewer and interviewee. Politeness was exhibited in many ways such as offering the interviewer a comfortable chair, offering refreshment, and walking the interviewer to her car. As has been stated, the Japanese American's concern for politeness should not be misinterpreted as

weakness. Instead, politeness is another manifestation of the collective orientation and *ninjo* (feeling of humanity).

6. *A tendency for understatement and an emphasis on non-verbal communication.* This theme is closely related to the emphasis on deference and politeness in that modesty of expression is also a way of being polite. For example, in the study, answers to questions concerned with finances often took a middle stance and were often understatements of poorer conditions on one hand or more wealthy environments on the other.

Non-verbal communication is also intertwined with the politeness of not being verbose and the indirectness of the Japanese pattern of communication. The Sapir-Whorf hypothesis suggests that the structure of a language predisposes its speaker to live in a particular reality. In the Japanese pattern of communication, not only is the language circulatory in construction, but words are considered to be only a tool and not the sole means of communication. Therefore, words are not to be taken at their face value and attention must be paid to non-verbal communication. (Kunihiro, 1973.)

Kunihiro (1973) provides the example of a Japanese person saying "I've already eaten," when asked if she/he would like something to eat. If the host takes the guest literally and doesn't try to persuade them to have something to eat anyway, the host stands a good chance of being criticized later for being insensitive or unconcerned. The host is supposed to make sure that the guest wasn't just being polite by saying something like, "Oh, come on. Join us anyway."

Selected References

Bosworth, A.R.   *America's concentration camps.* New York: Norton and Co., 1967.

Caudill, W.   General culture: The influence of social structure and culture on human behavior in modern Japan. *Journal of Nervous and Mental Disease,* 1973, *157* (4), 240-257.

——————   Japanese American personality and acculturation. *Genetic Psychology Monographs,* 1952, *45,* 7-15.

Chin, F.; Chan, J.P.; Inada, L.F.; & Wong, S.   *AIIIEEEEE!: An anthology of Asian writers.* Washington, D.C.: Howard University Press, 1974.

Gee, E.   Issei: The first women. In *Asian Women.* Berkeley: University of California, 1971.

Hatanaka, H.K.; Watanabe, B.Y.; & Ono, S.   The utilization of mental health services by Asian Americans in the Los Angeles area. In W.H. Ishikawa & N.H. Archer (Eds.) *Service delivery in Pan Asian communities.* San Diego, Calif.: San Diego Pacific Asian Coalition, 1975.

Iga, M.   The Japanese social structure and the source of mental strains of Japanese immigrants in the United States. *Social Forces,* 1967, *35,* 271-278.

Japanese American Citizen's League.   *The experience of Japanese Americans in the United States: A teacher resource manual.* San Francisco, 1975.

Kalish, R.A., & Moriwaki, S.   The world of the elderly Asian American. *Journal of Social Issues,* 1973, *29* (2), 187-209.

Kitano, H.H.L. *Japanese Americans: The evolution of a subculture.* Englewood Cliffs: Prentice-Hall, 1969.

Kunihiro, M. Indigenous barriers to communication. *The wheel extended,* 1974, *3* (4), 11-17.

Miyamoto, S.F. An immigrant community in America. In H. Conroy & T.S. Miyakawa. (Eds.) *East across the Pacific: Historical and sociological studies of Japanese immigration and assimilation.* Santa Barbara, Calif.: American Bibliographic Center, Clio Press, 1972.

_____. Social solidarity among the Japanese in Seattle. *University of Washington Publications in the Social Sciences,* 1939, *11* (2), 59-130.

Nishio, A. The Oriental as middleman minority. *Gidra,* May 1969, 3.

Okimoto, D. *American in disguise.* New York: John Weatherhill, Inc., 1971.

A study of selected socio-economic characteristics of ethnic minorities based on the 1970 census. Asian Americans Vol. 2. Office of Special Concerns, Office of the Assistant Secretary for Planning & Evaluation, HEW, July 1974.

APPENDIX B:
LITERATURE ON JAPANESE AMERICAN ELDERLY

The body of written knowledge on Japanese American aging per se remains scarce. Because of the general lack in the quantity and quality of written material specifically on Japanese American elderly, the bibliographic list that follows attempts to provide the reader with a broad reference list that might provide some knowledge and insight into Japanese American elderly.

From the field of social gerontology itself, published literature that includes material on Japanese American elderly is limited to works on Pacific Asian and minority elderly in general, (Bell, Kasschau, and Zellman, 1976; Institute on Minority Aging, 1974; Kalish and Moriwaki, 1973; Training Project for Asian Elderly, 1973; Kalish and Yuen, 1971; White House Conference, 1971). Academic material that specifically addresses Japanese American aging is primarily limited to unpublished papers and theses (Fujii, 1975; Kiefer, 1974; Kuramoto, 1971; Reynolds, 1971; Tamura, 1969; Endo and Yoshida, 1968; Staniford, 1961; Kanagawa, 1955).

The majority of the works listed in this appendix are cultural and sociohistorical in nature and are included because of their relevance to elderly Japanese Americans and because of the dearth of existing gerontological literature.

Two other important sources of literature on Japanese American elderly included are often overlooked and neglected by the social sciences. They are primary source materials written in Japanese (see Ichioka, Sakata, Tsuchida, and Yashuhara, 1974) and creative literature written by and about Japanese Americans represented by Takahashi (1975), Okada (1957), Sone (1953), and Mori (1949). These sources provide firsthand information and an inside perspective into the reality of the situations and experiences experienced by Japanese American older people.

A list of films reflective of elderly Japanese Americans is included as another important source of reference.

Books

Herman, M. (Ed.). *The Japanese in America 1843-1973 a chronology and fact book.* (Ethnic Chronology Series No. 15.) Dobbs Ferry, New York: Oceana Publications, Inc., 1974.

Hosokawa, B. *Nisei: The quiet Americans.* New York: William Morrow and Company, Inc., 1969.

Ichihashi, Y. *Japanese in the United States.* Stanford, Calif.: Stanford University Press, 1932.

Ichioka, Y.; Sakata, Y.; Tsuchida, N.; & Yasuhara, E. *A buried past: An annotated bibliography of the Japanese American research project.* Los Angeles: University of California Press, 1974.

Ito, K. *Issei: A history of Japanese immigrants in North America.* Seattle, Wash.: Japanese-American Community Services & Tokyo: Japan Publishers, 1973.

Kiefer, C.W. *Changing cultures, changing lives: An ethnographic study of three generations of Japanese Americans.* San Francisco: Jossey-Bass Publishers, 1974.

Kitagawa, D. *Issei and Nisei: The internment years.* New York: The Seabury Press, 1967.

Kitano, H.H.L. *Japanese Americans: The evolution of a subculture.* Englewood Cliffs: Prentice-Hall, 1969.

Maykovich, M.K. *Japanese American identity dilemma.* Tokyo: Waseda University Press, 1972.

Articles

Alexandre, M. The Nisei—a casualty of World War II. *Cornell Law Quarterly,* 1943, *28,* 385-413.

Arkoff, A. Need patterns in two generations of Japanese Americans in Hawaii. *Journal of Social Psychology,* 1959, *50,* 75-79.

Babcock, C.B., & Caudill, W. Personal and cultural factors in treating a Nisei man. In G. Seward (Ed.) *Studies in culture conflict.* New York: Ronald Press, 1958.

Berrien, F.K.; Arkoff, A.; & Iwahara, S. Generational difference in values: Americans, Japanese Americans, and Japanese. *The Journal of Social Psychology,* 1967, *71,* 169-175.

Bessent, T.E. An aging Issei anticipates rejection. In G. Seward (Ed.) *Clinical studies in culture conflict.* New York: Ronald Press, 1958.

Caudill, W., & DeVos, G. Achievement, culture and personality: The case of the Japanese Americans. *American Anthropologist,* 1956, *58,* 1102-1226.

Daniels, R. The Issei generation. In A. Tachiki, E. Wong, F. Odo, B. Wong (Eds.) *Roots: An Asian American reader.* Los Angeles: UCLA Asian American Studies Center, 1971.

Farbero, W.; Shneidman, L.; & Shneidman, E.S.   A Nisei woman attacks by suicide. In G. Seward (Ed.) *Clinical studies in culture conflict.* New York; Ronald Press, 1958.

Gee, E.   Issei: The first women. In *Asian Women.* Berkeley: University of California Press, 1971.

Hosokowa, B.   More Issei-ese. *Pacific Citizen,* 1975.

Iga, M.   The Japanese social structure and the source of mental strains of Japanese immigrants in the United States. *Social Forces,* 1967, *35,* 271-278.

_____   Do most Japanese living in the United States still retain traditional Japanese personality? *Kashu Mainichi.* Los Angeles, June 21, 1967.

Ito, A.   Keiro nursing home, a study of Japanese cultural adaptations. In E.P. Stanford (Ed.) *Minority Aging, First Institute Proceedings.* San Diego: San Diego State University, Center on Aging, 1974.

Kalish, R.A., & Moriwaki, S.   The world of the elderly Asian American. *Journal of Social Issues,* 1973, *29* (2), 187-209.

Kalish, R.A., & Yuen, S.   Americans of East Asian ancestry: Aging and the aged. *The Gerontologist,* 1971, *11,* 36-47.

Kitano, H.H.L.   Differential child-rearing attitudes between first and second generation Japanese in the United States. *Journal of Social Psychology,* 1961, *53,* 13-20.

_____   Japanese American mental illness. In S. Sue & N. Wagner (Eds.) *Asian American Psychological Perspectives.* Palo Alto: Science and Behavior Books, Inc., 1973.

Lyman, S.   Generation and character: The case of the Japanese Americans. In H. Conroy & T.S. Miyakawa (Eds.) *East across the Pacific.* Santa Barbara, Calif.: American Bibliographical Center, Clio Press, 1972.

Masuda, M.; Matsumoto, G.H.; & Meredith, G.M.   Ethnic identity in three generations of Japanese Americans. *Journal of Social Psychology,* 1910, *81,* 199-207.

Masuoka, J.   Race relations and Nisei problems. *Sociology and Social Research.* 1945, *30,* 452-459.

Miyamoto, S.F.   An immigrant community in America. In H. Conroy & T.S. Miyakawa (Eds.) *East across the Pacific.* Santa Barbara, Calif.: American Bibliographic Center, Clio Press, 1972.

_____   Social solidarity among the Japanese in Seattle. *University of Washington Publications in the Social Sciences,* 1939, *2* (2), 59-130.

Modell, J.   The Japanese American family: A perspective for future investigation. *Pacific Historical Review,* 1968, *36,* 67-81.

Olinger, L.B., & Sommers, V.S.   The divided path: Psychocultural neurosis in a Nisei man. In G. Seward (Ed.) *Clinical Studies in Culture Conflict.* New York: Ronald Press, 1958.

Opler. M.K.   Cultural dilemma of a Kibei youth. In G. Seward (Ed.) *Clinical studies in culture conflict.* New York: The Ronald Press, 1958.

Unpublished Works

Abe, S.K.   *Nisei personality characteristics as measured by the Edwards Personal Preference Schedule and Minnesota Multi-Phasic Personality Inventory.* Unpublished doctoral dissertation, University of Utah, 1958.

Cho, C.S.   *Correlation of cultural assimilation of two groups of Issei women.* Unpublished master's thesis, University of Washington, Seattle, 1953.

Endo, P., & Yoshida, J.   *An exploratory study of the impact of aging in the Japanese American family.* Unpublished master's thesis, University of Southern California, 1968.

Fujii, S.M.   *The accessibility of nursing homes to elderly Asian Americans.* Statement presented to the Subcommittee on Long-Term Care of the U.S. Senate Special Committee on Aging, Washington, D.C., August 10, 1972.

Fujii, S.M.   *An exploratory-descriptive study of socio-cultural barriers to health services utilization for elderly Japanese as perceived by middle aged and elderly Japanese Americans.* Unpublished doctoral dissertation, Brandeis University, 1975.

Hayashida, A.   *Japanese moral instruction as a factor in the Americanization of citizens of Japanese ancestry.* Unpublished master's thesis, University of Hawaii, 1933.

Ishizuka, K.C.   *"Wataridori: Birds of passage"—its significance for the field of social gerontology.* Paper accompanying the film, presented at the 28th Annual Meeting of the Gerontological Society, Louisville, Kentucky, October 1975.

Kanagawa, W.Y.   *A study of old age assistance recipients of Japanese ancestry under the Honolulu County, Department of Public Welfare, Territory of Hawaii.* Unpublished master's thesis, University of Hawaii, Honolulu, 1955.

Kiefer, C.W.   *The limitations of theory: A case report on the Japanese American elderly.* Paper presented at the 1974 Annual Meetings of the Gerontological Society, Portland, Oregon, October 28-November 1, 1974.

Kimura, Y.   *A comparative study of the collective adjustment of the Issei: The first generation Japanese in Hawaii and in mainland United States since Pearl Harbor.* Unpublished doctoral dissertation, University of Chicago, 1952.

Kuramoto, F.H.   *Aging among Japanese Americans.* Paper presented to University of Southern California, Gerontology Center Summer Institute on Ethnicity and Aging, Los Angeles, July 1971.

Kuramoto, F.H.   *Japanese aliens and public welfare in California: A current illustration.* Unpublished manuscript, University of Southern California, School of Social Work, May 1971.

Nakagaki, M.   *A study of marriage and family relationships among three generations of Japanese Americans.* Unpublished master's thesis, University of Southern California, 1964.

Owan, T.   *Asian Americans: Case of benighted neglect.* Paper presented to the National Conference on Social Welfare, San Francisco, May 1975.

Reynolds, D.L.   *Attitudes and consequences of death related behaviors in the Japanese American community.* Mimeo, June 1970.

Reynolds, D.L.   *Japanese American aging: A game perspective.* Paper presented at the Society for Applied Anthropology Meeting, Miami, Florida, 1971.

Ross, R. *Social distance between first and second generation Japanese in Los Angeles.* Unpublished master's thesis, University of Southern California, 1939.

Staniford, P.S. *Values of some Issei Japanese of Hanapepe Valley, Kauai.* Unpublished master's thesis, University of Hawaii, 1961.

Tamura, F.Y. *A cross-generational study of the attitudes toward the aging person and aging process and the acceptance of a 'home for the aged' in the Japanese American elderly.* Unpublished master's thesis, University of California, Los Angeles, 1969.

Yangita, Y. *Familial, occupational and social characteristics of three generations of Japanese Americans.* Unpublished master's thesis, University of Southern California, 1969.

Documents

Akagi, R.H. *The second generation problem.* The Japanese Students Christian Association in North America, June 1926.

The Asian American elderly. Reports of the Special Concerns Sessions, 1971 White House Conference on Aging. Washington, D.C.: U.S. Government Printing Office, 1971.

Asian Americans and Pacific peoples: A case of mistaken identity. A report prepared by the California Advisory Committee to the United States Commission on Civil Rights, February 1975.

Bell, D., Kassachau, P., & Zellman, G. *Delivering services to elderly members of minority groups: A critical review of the literature.* Santa Monica: Rand Corporation, 1976.

Californians of Japanese, Chinese and Pilipino ancestry: Population, employment, income, education. San Francisco: State of California, Department of Industrial Relations, Division of Fair Employment Practices, June 1965.

Japanese American Citizen's League. *The experience of Japanese Americans in the United States: A teacher resource manual.* San Francisco, 1975.

Training Project for the Asian Elderly. *On the feasibility of training Asians to work with Asian elderly: A preliminary assessment of needs and resources available to Asian elderly in Seattle, Washington, 1973.*

Creative Literature

Mori, T. *Yokohama, California.* Caldwell, Idaho: Caxton Printers, 1949.

Okada, J. *No-no boy.* Rutland, Vermont: Charles E. Tuttle, 1957.

Sone, M. *Nisei daughter.* Boston: Little, Brown and Company, 1953.

Takahashi, F. Nisei, Nisei. In L. Faderman & B. Bradshaw (Eds.) *Speaking for ourselves: American ethnic writing.* Glenview, Ill.: Scott, Foresman and Company, 1975.

_____ The widower. In L. Faderman & B. Bradshaw (Eds.) *Speaking for ourselves: American ethnic writing.* Glenview, Ill.: Scott, Foresman and Company, 1975.

Films

Nisei: The pride and the shame.   CBS Twentieth Century Series.
Issei, Nisei, Sansei.   New Jersey Public Broadcasting.
Issei: The first fifty years.   UCLA Asian American Studies Center.
Wataridori: Birds of passage.   Los Angeles: Visual Communications.